# *EZRA POUND*

*Modern  Literature  Monographs*

# EZRA POUND

*Jeannette Lander*

*Frederick Ungar Publishing Co.*
*New York*

Published by arrangement with Colloquium Verlag, Berlin.
Translated from the original German, and revised, by the
author.

# Contents

## ACKNOWLEDGMENTS

The following excerpts, reprinted by permission of New Directions Publishing Corporation, from EZRA POUND, *Personae*, copyright 1926 by Ezra Pound; *The Cantos*, copyright 1937, 1948 by Ezra Pound; *The Selected Letters of Ezra Pound*, copyright 1950 by Ezra Pound; *Literary Essays of Ezra Pound*, copyright 1918, 1920, 1935 by Ezra Pound; *Gaudier-Brzeska, a Memoir*, copyright 1970 by Ezra Pound; *ABC Reading*, All rights reserved; from HUGH KENNER, *The Poetry of Ezra Pound*, All rights reserved; from FORREST READ, ED. *Pound/Joyce*, copyright 1965, 1966, 1967 by Ezra Pound.

# 1

*Facets*

"The kindest-hearted man who ever cut a throat." Ford Madox Ford's characterization of Ezra Pound[1] only hints at the paradoxical nature of certainly the most controversial figure in twentieth-century American letters.

The question is most often asked about this paradox of a person: Is Ezra Pound an anti-Semite? He was one of the earliest admirers and translators in America of the German-Jewish poet Heinrich Heine, and it is no doubt a genuine sentiment that Pound expressed in one of his poems of this period:

> O Harry Heine, curses be,
> I live too late to sup with thee!
> Who can demolish at such polished ease
> Philista's pomp and Art's pomposities![2]

This little four-liner contains not only Poundian humor but also Poundian esteem. Pound has also been persevering in his support of the Jewish poet Louis Zukofsky. In fact, he dedicated his book *Guide to Kulchur* to him as late as 1938, which was almost twenty years after the publication of his first articles on economy in which he identified world Jewry with usury—to Pound the greatest malady of mankind—and more than ten years after his emigration to Italy and his first publications in support of Italian Fascism. Zukofsky wrote in 1946:

I never felt the least trace of anti-Semitism in his presence. Nothing he ever said to me made me feel the embarrassment I always have for the "Goy" in whom a residue of antagonism for the "Jew" remains. If we had an occasion to use the word "Jew" and "Goy" they were no more or less ethnological in their sense than "Chinese" and "Italian."[3]

Statements that Pound himself has made, however, are in stark contrast to Zukofsky's assertion. In a letter (1922) to Harriet Monroe, for example, he writes:

"Damn remnants in you of Jew religion, that bitch Moses and the rest of the tribal barbarians."[4] Beyond such direct outbursts, there are in Pound's letters the numerous statements in which he seeks to negate altogether, or at least to discredit, the Jewish element in Christianity. "To hell wiff [sic] Abraham. Most of the constructive so-called Xtn ideas are out of the Stoics. In fact, I should suggest that *all* 'Christian decency' is sheer stoic. I doubt if any single ethical idea now honoured comes from Jewry."[5] Or: "Christianity is (or was when real) anti-Semitism."[6] And: "All the Jew part of the Bible is black evil."[7]

Such statements, when uttered by a poet of Pound's rank and influence, cannot be disregarded, especially when the expressed sentiments or convictions speak out of the poet's works as well. Pound's lifework, the *Cantos,* revolves around the idea of an all-devouring usury. This usury is the great evil power that perverts the natural fertility of mankind and the earth. It destroys the original mystery that links the divine and the human. In the *Cantos* Pound indifferently allows "Rothschild" to stand for this great destructive power (*Canto XLVI,* for instance). Or "David rex," whom he dubs the prime son of a bitch (*Canto LXXIV*).

Nonetheless, the question of Pound's anti-Semitism is not one to be answered with a categoric "yes" or "no," nor is it answerable at all without due consideration of biographical facts. It can be answered only specifically. That is to say, Pound can certainly have entertained a positive opinion of individual Jewish persons without contradicting his ideological anti-Semitism. In the age of Fascism, it was not a rare thing to flaunt personal Jewish friendships while denouncing the Jews as a people. The question of Pound's anti-Semitism has for apparent reasons been pushed into the foreground again and again. Although

it is inseparable from the greater ideological complex
of the age, more precisely from the ideology of Fascism
in all its diverse forms, it has been viewed an isolated
phenomenon. Anti-Semitism is by no means the only
paradoxical aspect of Pound's personality to be considered. If Pound vacillated between two ostensibly
incompatible positions, personal friendship and ideological hatred for Jewry, this is typical of his entire
mode of existence. Vacillation between opposites, even
between extremes, is inevitably a part of his aesthetics
as well. It is simply an excursion between good and evil.

There are masterful passages in Pound's work
and those that can only be called banal. There are
verses that are rich in meaning and others that are—at
least on the surface—incoherent. And there is the fact
that with the years Pound's poetic language became increasingly impenetrable.

Ezra Pound had, quite early in his career, begun
using Latin terms, concepts out of Greek philosophy,
and quotations from the troubadour lyrics of the
Provence and from Italian literature (Dante); in the
*Cantos,* his late work, there are Chinese ideograms, the
names of obscure theorists in economics, the nicknames
of unnamed personal friends, and local place names
out of personal memory. The question that presents
itself on reading the *Cantos* for the first time is whether
or not such a method of "poetry-writing" does not directly contradict those principles that Pound himself
called the guiding principles of modern poetry. The
precise word for the exact meaning to be conveyed—
for Ezra Pound this is the criterion of poetry.

Poetry must be *as well written as prose.* Its language must be a
fine language, departing in no way from speech save by height-
ened intensity (i.e. simplicity). There must be no book words, no
periphrases, no inversions. It must be as simple as De Maupas-
sant's best prose, and as hard as Stendhal's.[8]

For Pound, an elementary tool in the handicraft of the poet is the mastery of both the natural melody and the cadence of language as they are dependent on the sense of the words and the mood of the whole. By the same token, the ability to recite such poetry melodically and rhythmically must also be elementary. But Pound himself was not adept in, for instance, the pronunciation of Chinese and had only an imperfect knowledge of the range of definition and association of the very ideograms he uses.

Contradictions in Pound's character are as manifest as in his work. On the one hand, he is the discoverer and altruistic supporter of T. S. Eliot and James Joyce, to name only two. (For months in a row he carried on a selfless campaign, writing petitionary letters and collecting funds, just to get these authors into print.) On the other hand, as in the case of Robert Frost, he reveals himself as the offended impresario and claims in a letter to the *Boston Transcript* all the credit for Frost's literary success in England, as though it had been Ezra Pound alone who fostered that success.

And what about the literary movements that Pound founded or to which he gave the decisive impetus, only to leave them again after a time? Are not the principles of, for example, the imagists directly contrary to such generalizations as Pound himself has made about them, calling Shakespeare an imagist or attributing some Japanese poems to the imagist school?

How shall we consider the Ezra Pound who couldn't carry a tune and yet composed two operas? How shall we consider the Ezra Pound who often and convincingly expounded his firm belief in American democracy and yet gave the American government reason to raise charges of treason against him?

Pound would be the last person to sanction an evaluation of his work that is in any way based on biographical data. "You can spot the bad critic when he starts by discussing the poet and not the poem," he says in *ABC of Reading*.[9] The poetic works of Ezra Pound, however, leave the critic no other possibility but to consider the life of Ezra Pound. The *Cantos* are not seldom a catalogue of Pound's studies, acquaintances, and experiences. In *Canto LXXIX,* for example, he writes: "So Astafieva had considered the tradition /From Byzance and before then." To understand Pound's thought here, it is essential to know that Astafieva was a Russian ballet dancer whom Pound had met (in London in 1918) and whose work he considered masterly.

The Pound scholar John Edwards has compiled a reference book for the *Cantos* that lists quotations, names, place names, elements that appear in foreign languages, et cetera, and explains them all: *The Annotated Index to the Cantos of Ezra Pound,* a book, says Pound, for uneducated people. With the help of this index, one can approach the *Cantos* as though they were a crossword puzzle. Much the better method, however, is to approach Pound's work historically or at least chronologically, that is, to trace it from its beginnings and to follow the development of Poundian thought.

Where do his ideas come from? How has he used them? How has he changed them into peculiarly Poundian ideas? What does he want to tell us with his poems, with the *Cantos* in particular? Is Pound a great poet or a charlatan? An artist or an impostor? Are the Poundian paradoxes real or only apparent? To answer these questions and to approach an understanding of this poet's work, we must follow the growth of his ideas from their incipience. There is only one statement that can safely be made about his work even without such an analysis: Pound led English and American poetry into the modern era. This is an established fact in literary history. It is our reason for undertaking whatever other evaluations there are to be made, that is, of Pound's ostensive revolution in lyrical language, or of his allegedly eruptive and raving hatred of the Jews. These phenomena must be investigated objectively and methodically, beginning at the roots and tracing consequent developments.

Going back to the roots is a Poundian principle. It manifests itself in his search for the natural language, the original religion, the sources of art. Through all the facets of his paradoxical being, one can trace Pound's struggle to know the highest achievements of human culture from the source and to understand the very spirit out of which they were born, so that he and all modern artists might be more capable of creating works of the highest order.

# 2

*Pioneer
Spirit*

Ezra Pound was born on October 30, 1885, in the first plaster residence of the log-house settlement of Hailey, Idaho. The settlement is situated in the valley of the Snake River, which has its source in the heights of the Rocky Mountains that everywhere surround the valley and which flows into the great Columbia River. In 1885, this region was still pioneer country; the first white men to set foot in it, the famed explorers Lewis and Clark, had done so only eighty years before. The first building in Idaho, a trading post for fur-trappers, was built in 1810.

Through the Snake River valley ran the Oregon Trail, the storied road of the white men and women who settled the American West. The first hundred of these pioneers had begun their long trek in 1842. In the next year, another wagon train, this time with a full thousand of the daring, traveled that arduous way.

After that large migration, the number of pioneers rose quickly. But aside from those who died on the way and were buried there, none remained in the state of Idaho. Only after gold was discovered there in 1860 did the permanent settlement of Idaho begin. In 1890, all of Idaho, an area as large as England and Scotland combined, had only 88,548 inhabitants.

The pioneer spirit of these frontiersmen influenced Ezra Pound, even though he was still a very small child when his family moved East. His father had been a government employee in the land office in which newly staked-out claims had to be registered. In 1888, he was transferred to Pennsylvania as assayer in the mint. By that time, what can be called a frontier spirit had long been an integral part of family tradition. Ezra Pound's grandfather had helped to lay the first railroad through the then quite wild West and had been a lumberjack in the virgin forests of Wisconsin before he was elected a Representative and sent to Washington. Ezra Pound was always conscious of his frontiersman heritage. In 1917, he wrote from London to his friend William Carlos Williams, who was born in New Jersey, had spent his whole life in that vicinity, and whose mother was of Spanish origin:

And America! What the hell do you a bloomin' foreigner know about the place? Your père only penetrated the edge, and you've never been west of Upper Darby . . . My dear boy, you have never felt the whoop of the PEEraries. You have never seen the projecting and protuberant Mts. of the Sierra Nevada. WOT can you know of the country? . . .
But I (der grosse Ich) have the virus, the bacillus of the land in my blood, for nearly three bleating centuries.[1]

Of course, these lines are full of the self-irony that is typical of Pound, but the very nature of self-irony is that it is based on a core of truth. And the correspondence between Williams and Pound at this time is marked by its frankness and genuine mutual respect. The friendship between the two poets began when they were fellow students at the University of Pennsylvania, and for a period of over fifty years, it withstood the rupturing effects of egocentrism and individualism (traits common to both parties), of petty quarrels and differences of opinion.

Pound enrolled at the University of Pennsylvania at the age of fifteen, after having spent a sheltered and proper childhood in the little Eastern town of Wyncote, Pennsylvania. The white two-story wooden house, with its porch and garden and, for this section of the country, typical gables, is still standing in what is now a well-cared-for and well-to-do suburb. Pound's parents were middle-class people who, despite all their frontier tradition, were not prone to differ much from their middle-class neighbors. The conformity, which Pound was later to dramatically, if not theatrically, renounce, afforded him, during his childhood at least, a secure environment. He and his parents enjoyed a good relationship, a mutual understanding that remained constant through the years. The father, who took a realistic and pragmatic view of things, was always the best counselor for the eccentric son of whom he was so proud. He was certain that his increasing incomprehensibility of Ezra's poems was due to his son's burgeoning knowledge. In his letters to his son, he posed questions that would help him to bridge the gap of knowledge and to understand. Ezra always tried to answer his father's questions. At times, the correspondence led the poet to reappraise the preciseness of his choice of words. Nowhere in these letters is there an allusion to his father's education, though Pound was on every other occasion ready to make a pungent and sarcastic allusion to the "education" of friend and foe.

Education had always played a major role in Pound's life. Although he began his own very early, he seldom pursued it for the purposes that are generally accepted. As a fifteen-year-old student at the university, he was already conspicuous for his individuality of judgment. He had no "major" and no "minor" subjects, but chose to enroll as a "special student," that is, as a student who does not take courses with the aim of fulfilling requirements for a degree, who indeed does not wish to acquire a degree. He signed up only for courses that were of interest to him. When, after two years, this manner of studying began to irritate the university faculty, Pound transferred to Hamilton College in upstate New York. While there, he maintained his friendship with William Carlos Williams and other students at the University of Pennsylvania through correspondence. Three years later, he returned to the university as a graduate student.

At this time, a young girl by the name of Hilda

Doolittle was a student at the nearby Bryn Mawr College for girls. The sensitive, well-bred, and striking daughter of a professor became Pound's first serious romantic interest. When Pound asked her father for her hand in marriage, the professor only answered that to him he, Pound, was little more than a nomad. Hilda remained one of Pound's closest friends for many years. She was with him in London for a time. Their engagement to be married came to naught. Later, as H. D., she was one of the most talented of the imagist poets.

Pound was also engaged to Frances Gregg, but none of his acquaintances at the time knew anything about it. How secretive Pound was in regard to his friendships with women is best illustrated by the dedication in his book of poems *Personae*. From the date the book was first published in 1909 up to the present time, this dedication has been printed in every edition: "This book is for Mary Moore of Trenton, if she wants it." Who, however, Mary Moore of Trenton was or is has remained a mystery. William Carlos Williams said she might be one of the two girls whom he and Pound met at a school on Chestnut Hill; Pound only mentioned that he had entered her house through a French window.

Both Hamilton College and the University of Pennsylvania were of the greatest significance in Pound's further development. At the former, where Pound received his Bachelor of Arts degree, he studied Romance languages under William Pierce. Pierce, having been a student in Heidelberg and at the Sorbonne, instilled in Pound what became a lasting love for the world of Dante and the troubadours. At the University of Pennsylvania where he received his Master's degree, Pound came under the influence of Hugo A. Rennert, professor of Romance languages and biographer of Lope de Vega. Allusions to these men and anecdotes about them that speak of their importance to him are to be found in Pound's prose and even in the very late Cantos.

It was through the efforts of Pierce and Rennert that Pound was able to go to France in 1906 as a "Fellow in Romance Languages" with a scholarship to do research on, and translate the works of Lope de Vega. He was twenty-one years old when he arrived in the Provence.

Here Pound began an intensive inquiry into the medieval language and poetry of the troubadours, a pursuit that he has never since put aside and that has been a major source for his work. The troubadours became the subject matter of his early poems. It was in the course of mastering their language that Pound learned the poetic possibilities and impossibilities of his own. In the melodies of their songs, Pound discovered for himself what lyric music is. These songs are Pound's criteria for good poetry.

At such an early age, Pound refused to accept without question as "great" those works that learned men and traditional anthologies have passed down to us as such. In this type of hand-me-down veneration, he sees the danger that generation after generation uncritically accept criteria for "greatness" that are no longer unchallengeable, that works having only historical significance continue to be honored as "timeless." Instead of always reading *about* such works, Pound says, we must begin to read and to judge the works themselves.

In Europe Pound began, without the restrictions and without the aid of the university, to read the works of the troubadours, and these, whenever possible, in the original. In Milan, he rediscovered unpublished manuscripts by Arnaut Daniel, a Provençal troubadour poet. Pound began translating Daniel's poems then. He translated them, adapted them to the English language, and retranslated them through the next seventeen years. Not only because he was a thorough worker but also because he had developed a genuine love for these poems, Pound began to wander over the Provençal countryside that is their locale. He measured the distances between the castles and compared the historical facts that can be reconstructed with the stories told in the poems. His thoughts and experiences during these excursions found expression in two of his own poems, "Provincia Deserta" and "Near Perigord."

However, it is not so much on the subject matter of his poetry as on his poetic technique that these Provençal studies had a lasting influence. In his essay "How I Began," Pound describes the coming into being of "Sestina Altaforte," an adaptation of a Provençal poem by Bertran de Born:

I wanted the curious involution and recurrence of the Sestina. I knew more or less of the arrangement. I wrote the first strophe and then went to the museum to make sure of the right order of the permutations, . . . I did the rest of the poem at a sitting. Technically it is one of my best.[2]

With these attempts to render fully the intrinsic beauty of Provençal verse to a reading public that had no linguistic basis for its appreciation, Pound first began his training in the mastery of form, rhythm, and sound. And this mastery was for the young Pound, for the lyric poet, prerequisite to the attainment of music in verse.

Pound came of a family that appreciated classical European music and in which it was not uncommon for members who knew an instrument to play together of an evening. William Carlos Williams and William Butler Yeats have both testified that Pound could not

carry a tune; nevertheless, his childhood experience
had given him a musical knowledge quite beyond that
of most Americans of his generation. For Pound, the
need to continue his musical education went hand in
hand with attainment of formal musical mastery in
poetic language. In "Vers Libre and Arnold Dolmetsch," Pound writes:

Poetry is a composition of words set to music. . . . The propor-
tion or quality of the music may, and does, vary; but poetry
withers and "dries out" when it leaves music, or at least imagined
music, too far behind it . . . Poets who are not interested in
music are, or become, bad poets. . . . Poets who will not study
music are defective.[3]

Such thoughts about the history, subject matter,
and technique of poetry, although he set them down at
later dates (he wrote the above in 1917), have their
origin, as Pound himself has said, in his study of the
troubadours between 1903 and 1906. His troubadour
quests took him not only through France but also to
Spain and Italy.

Pound made an effort to convince the University
of Pennsylvania of the fruitfulness of his European
sojourn and of the necessity of having his research
grant renewed, but the University turned his request
down. Pound returned to the United States and successfully applied for a position at Wabash College in
Crawfordsville, Illinois (1907). With his acceptance
there, he was "stranded in a most godforsakenest area
of the Middle West," as he writes in *Patria Mia.*[4]

A pioneer spirit was no longer alive in Crawfordsville. And at no time did Pound experience there the
feeling that the great wide plains held unlimited possibilities, or that the land still waited for the inquisi-
tive, the courageous, or the bold in spirit. Nor was
there any fertile ground for culture. Crawfordsville
was to Pound "the sixth circle of desolation."[5]

Pound entitled a poem that he wrote in 1907 "In Durance"—an allusion to "imprisonment" and a pun on "endurance." Despite his isolation in Crawfordsville, Pound could probably have "endured" it if it had not been for a certain splitting of the American personality that took place in the wake of Puritanism, which prevails for the most part in provincial areas, and that put an end to his Wabash career after four short months.

In his search for people of kindred spirit, Pound invited actors and actresses of itinerant troupes to his rooms. He wrote to a friend that he would no doubt have trouble with the college authorities on this account.

Not long afterward, he met on the street a dancing girl from a show that had recently passed through. She had neither money nor a room, so Pound bought her a meal and let her spend the night at his apartment. She slept on his bed, and he slept on the floor. Thinking no more about it, he left for college as usual early the next morning.

His landladies, two unmarried sisters named Hall, discovered the girl still asleep and informed the college president immediately; Pound was suspended without notice. His explanation of the affair was deemed insufficient. The grounds for his dismissal, as they originally were documented, "too European and too unconventional," were later eradicated, but it remains on record that Pound was a "Latin-Quarter type," this incompatible with a teaching position at Wabash. His dismissal was a turning point in his life, the turning-point between teaching and poetry, and between America and Europe.

An evaluation of "In Durance" makes it quite clear at what stage in his development as a poet Pound stood in 1907. There is no outstanding qualitative difference between this poem and the general run of contemporary verse; and poetry in the English language in that day stood at a very low level.

The Georgian poets were in vogue in England. The young James Joyce was writing academically conservative verse, and even this was unknown. William Butler Yeats had not yet thrown off the shackles of aestheticism.

In America, the picture was even more gloomy. Louis Untermeyer classifies the period as "Interim: 1890–1912."[6] The verse-makers of the time are now as well as forgotten. "In Durance" is both in diction and form a product of that epoch. Pound uses archaic personal pronouns, "thee" and "thou," as well as the corresponding biblical verb endings, "eth" as in "cometh," without inner poetic necessity, but because they belong to what was then accepted poetic diction. He reverses the natural order of the words, a "poetic" practice that he later specifically rejects. On the whole, he does not escape a romanticized tone and uses too many expressions that can only be called clichés. That he successfully employs free rhythm and does not cater to the current usage of rhyme in verse is not sufficient counterbalance to render "In Durance" a forerunner of modern poetry. Only two elements that are significant of Pound's later style find entry into his poetry of this period: prose quotations within the verse and foreign words or phrases left in the language of their origin. As for the rest, Pound had to undergo some stern self-training to become a "modern poet." In contrast to T. S. Eliot, for example, who wrote modern poetry whenever he wrote, Pound struggled for many years to free himself of the shackles of pre-Raphaelite conceptions.

He was his own guide and teacher in this process,

for as early as 1907 he knew what he wanted to achieve and had a clear idea of how to go about it.

I knew at fifteen pretty much what I wanted to do. I believed that the "Impulse" is with the gods, that technique is a man's own responsibility . . . a man is or is not a great poet. It is his own fault if he does not become a good artist—even a flawless artist.

I resolved that at thirty I would know more about poetry than any man living, that I would know the dynamic content from the shell, . . . what part of poetry was "indestructible," what part could *not be lost* by translation . . . what effects were attainable in *one* language only and were utterly incapable of being translated.

In this search I learned more or less nine foreign languages, I read Oriental stuff in translations, I fought every university regulation and every professor who tried to make me learn anything except this or who bothered me with "requirements for degrees."

Of course, no amount of scholarship will help a man write poetry, it may even be regarded as a great burden and hindrance, but it does help him to destroy a certain percentage of his failures. It keeps him discontented with mediocrity.[7]

Pound was quite serious about this plan for self-education. He returned to Europe—to "the source." That he did so was quite in keeping with his natural drive to perfect both his knowledge and his craftsmanship. The decision to do so, however, meant a deliberate suppression of another compulsion that was just as strong in him, the need to teach. T. S. Eliot, in his numerous comments on Pound, has often referred to this teaching urge as a "passion." Pound's abandonment of his teaching career can only be evaluated as a grave negation of his self-image as a deliberate break with what he knew to be a "calling." That his abilities in this field had gone unrecognized had shaken his faith in the university system in general. It was not simply a case of wounded vanity. Hardly a friend or

acquaintance of Pound's and later hardly a Pound
scholar has overlooked his genius as a teacher. Typical
is the opinion of Harriet Monroe, who, as the editor
of *Poetry* magazine, worked together with Pound for
many years.

Ezra Pound was born to be a great teacher. The American uni-
versities, which, at the time of his developing strength failed, one
and all, to install him as head of an English department, missed
a dynamic influence which would have been felt wherever English
writing is taught. It is not entirely his fault if he has become
somewhat embittered.[8]

After this breach, Pound never quite regained an
objective view of the world of teaching. On the contrary, he begins at this point a personal campaign,
which was to gain momentum and importance in the
course of his activities, against "institutionalized learning," which he deems a destructive force of every young
impulse in the arts. Now famous in literary circles is a
letter that Pound wrote in answer to a circular letter
from the Alumni Association of the University of
Pennsylvania. It documents, with a diction peculiar
only to Ezra Pound, his attitude toward the university
system.

Sir: Your circular letter of April 8 is probably excusable as a
circular letter. If it were a personal letter I shd. be obliged to
correct it.

Any news that the grad. school or any other "arts" segment of
the U. of P. had started to take an interest in civilization or "the
advancement of knowledge" or any other matter of interest wd.
be of interest.

The matter of keeping up one more otiose institution in a retro-
grade country seems to me to be the affair of those still bam-
boozled by mendicancy, rhetoric, and circular letters.

In other words what the HELL is the grad. school doing and

what the HELL does it think it is there for and when the hell
did it do anything but try to perpetuate the routine and stupidity that it was already perpetuating in 1873?
P.S. All the U. of P. or your god damn college or any other god
damn American college does or will do for a man of letters is ask
him to go away without breaking the silence . . .9

Pound's decision to take up residence in Europe
is not to be misinterpreted as resignation in the cause
of American arts. He writes in *Patria Mia* that he be-
lieves in the immanence of an American Renaissance.
Not only did he remain true to this belief, he set his
great store of energy to the work of bringing it about.
Pound wanted to create in America an atmosphere in
which the arts would thrive, but he was convinced
that the best way to do this was first to educate himself in Europe. He could not overlook the fact that the
America of 1908 was so far from the brink of this
Renaissance that it had neither eye nor ear for his
message.

My "career" has been of the simplest; during the first five years
of it I had exactly one brief poem accepted by one American
magazine, although I had during that time submitted "La
Fraisne" and various other poems now held as part of my best
work. Net result of my activities in cash, five dollars which works
out to about 4 S. 3 d. per year.10

Pound left the United States in January 1908.
Wabash had paid the remainder of his salary for the
current semester. His father had contributed a small
sum because some letters in praise of his son's poems
from the editors of *McClure's* magazine had convinced
him of the necessity of supporting a promising family
talent. Pound took a cattle boat and landed in Gi-
braltar. He had eighty dollars, some unpublished

poems, the unalterable intention of seeing those poems
in print, and the determination to reach London by
the shortest possible route.

# 3
# Masks

For Ezra Pound, Spain was as much "unexplored territory" as was the Wild West for his ancestors. And quite in keeping with the spirit of those ancestors, that is, to combine the adventure of new discovery with the practical consideration of commercial interests, he set about exploring the peninsula. Shortly after arriving, he met an American couple who confessed they were on a European tour for the first time and were unable to choose from such innumerable sights. Pound offered to be their guide for a small fee, bought with his first payment a reliable and comprehensive guidebook, prepared himself thoroughly before every excursion, and successfully played the role of an experienced tourist of Spain. Since he, too, was seeing the sights for the first time, he brought to each tour a spontaneous enthusiasm that must have been a delight to the couple he was guiding.

Several literary scholars have accused Pound of not knowing enough about the subjects he considers in his poems. But even as a very young man Pound had confidence in his ability quickly and correctly to recognize the crux of any matter and could trust his own judgment as to what was its essence and what its periphery. His experience as a guide in Spain is an example of such confidence. Though grotesque on the one hand, it was honest and certainly successful on the other. Pound had the courage to *act* in situations that were at the best difficult and at the worst hopeless. His journey to London from the "sticks" of the U.S. should be seen in this light.

The first stop on his way was Venice. He traveled there for the most part by foot in order to save his money for another, to him more important, purpose; and that was to pay for the printing of his poems. He knew that an acquaintance of his was in Venice at the time, Katherine Ruth Heyman, a pianist who was

in Europe on tour. Pound was rather a passionate ad-
mirer of Miss Heyman, who was fifteen years his
senior. He even at one point wrote to a friend that he
had abandoned his career as a poet to manage her
concert tours.

He did indeed send out press notices for a number
of her concerts, arrange a few others, and arrive in
London with her—as he later put it, more or less under
her wing. Katherine Heyman, who is referred to as
K. H. in *Canto LXXVI*—a canto Pound wrote some
thirty years later—was the dynamic and fascinating
daughter of a Jewish merchant and a woman whose
family had been among the founding fathers of America. Although Pound was infatuated, he had not, or
had not for long, serious intentions of giving up poetry. The poems he brought with him from the States
were printed in Venice in 1908 at his own cost. It was
his first book, quite a thin volume, *A Lume Spento*
("with candles quenched"). The title is a quotation
from Dante's *Purgatory* in the *Divine Comedy* and is
dedicated to a friend, William Brooke Smith, a talented young painter whom Pound had known at the
university and who died of tuberculosis at the age of
twenty-five. Thirteen years after Smith's death, Pound
wrote in a letter to William Carlos Williams: "At any
rate, thirteen years are gone; I haven't replaced him
and shant and no longer hope to."[1]

*A Lume Spento* was printed by A. Antonini, in an
edition of one hundred copies that were to be sold at
the price of five lire apiece. In 1948, forty years later,
one of the original copies was sold at auction for 150.00
dollars; a signed copy brought an auctioneer in London seventy-five pounds in 1957. The hundred copies
were for the most part not sold at all. Pound gave them
away, some to his friends (William Carlos Williams
and H. D. found very few words of praise for the

opus), some to well-known literary figures (for instance,
William Butler Yeats, whom Pound deemed the greatest living poet and who found the poems "charming").
Pound sent quite a number of copies to magazines and
newspapers for review.

The critics were unanimously of the opinion that
Pound's poems were "something different." The *Evening Standard* wrote, "Wild and haunting stuff . . .
coming after the trite and decorous stuff of most of our
decorous poets, this poet seems like a minstrel of
Provence at a suburban musical evening."[2] Pound was
classified as an American "original." In London, he
did everything he could to live up to this reputation.
William Carlos Williams once said, "Before meeting
Ezra Pound is like B.C. and A.D."[3] That precisely was
the impression Pound made in English literary circles.

It was only a matter of time in London, however,
until he had no money left. His father liked to tell the
story of Pound's enterprise in altering this situation.
Pound went to London Polytechnic Institute and introduced himself. "Would you like to enroll as a student?" he was asked. "No," he answered, "as a teacher.
I would like to lecture on Southern European Romance Literature." "But we have no need for a course
on that subject," he was told. "And besides, who are
you?" "Let me lecture," said Pound, "and you'll see
who I am."

Pound was hired. He received a very small salary
and taught at London Polytechnic for two years. This
episode, however, cannot be looked on as a return to
the teaching profession. Rather, it was a temporary
job until he could establish himself as a poet. Toward
that end, he directed all of his remarkable energies. It
appeared to Pound to be of the greatest importance
that a second volume of poems, no matter how thin,
follow as quickly as possible upon the first. He com-

piled a manuscript of some twenty-seven pages, *A Quinzaine for this Yule,* that was published shortly before Christmas 1908 by Pollock and Co. Pound himself probably bore the publishing costs for the edition of one hundred copies. That the cost of printing was relatively low in Europe had been a contributing factor toward Pound's decision to take up residence abroad. While an unknown poet in the U.S. at that time had to pay at least a thousand dollars for the printing of even a very small volume of poems, it cost Pound only eight dollars to have *A Lume Spento* printed in Venice.

Pound showed himself adept at utilizing self-advertisement to counterbalance the apparent lack of volume of his new book. In a critique in *The Bookman,* the comment appeared, "The smallness of his output does not indicate barrenness or indolence, but that he has a faculty of self-criticism; he has written and burned two novels and three hundred sonnets."[4] Pound had certainly supplied this information himself. Nowhere else do we find any reference to said novels; the sonnets, which he used to read to his friends at the university, he had really burned.

Actually, Pound's prose work consists only of critical writing. There is no fiction. The first critical essay that is known bears the date February 1909 and is a personal laudation of Walt Whitman.

He *is* America. His crudity is an exceeding great stench, but it *is* America. He is the hollow place in the rock that echos with his time. He *does* "chant the crucial stage" and he is the "voice triumphant." He is disgusting. He is an exceedingly nauseating pill, but he accomplishes his mission. Entirely free from the renaissance humanist ideal of the complete man or from the Greek idealism, he is content to be what he is, and he is his time and his people. He is a genius because he has vision of what he is and of his function. He knows that he is a beginning and not a classically finished work.[5]

It may have been a consequence of Pound's strong inclination toward Whitman that he now began to accentuate his role as an American "outsider" through his outward appearance and manner of living. Again and again in the accounts of his acquaintances in London at this time, such words as "conspicuous," "Bohemian," "Byronesque," and "bizarre" appear. Ford Madox Ford, who very soon became Pound's publisher, backer, and friend, gives the following description:

Ezra had a forked red beard, luxuriant chestnut hair, an aggressive lank figure; one long single stone earring dangled on his jawbone. He wore a purple hat, a green shirt, a black velvet coat, vermilion socks, openwork, brilliantly tanned sandals, and trousers of green billiard cloth in addition to an immence flowing tie that had been hand painted by a Japanese Futurist poet.[6]

Almost as soon as he arrived in London, Pound deliberately set about making the acquaintance of leading personalities in cultural circles. He once wrote that he had known all his life a hunger for interesting people. Good conversation was a matter of importance to him. He wanted to know the men whose work he valued. For these purposes, he used the old London clubs with literary tradition. He appeared at the monthly dinner of the "Square Club," which was founded by Chesterton, and among whose members were John Galsworthy, John Masefield, Walter de la Mare, as well as many influential critics. Not long afterward, Pound attended the Thursday evenings of the "Rhymers' Club" at "Ye Olde Cheshire Cheese" restaurant.

In these rooms on Fleet Street, Dr. Samuel Johnson had in his day held court. Now the best-known exponents of Irish literature met there: Yeats, Lionel Johnson, Sturge Moore, and Ernest Rhys. Pound's friend Ford liked to introduce young members into this club, and Pound was his "discovery." (Another discovery of Ford's was David Herbert Lawrence.) In the *Cantos,* much later, Pound maintains that the only great writer he had missed at this time was Swinburne.[7]

This intercourse with writers was not merely a superficial flirtation with literary society: for Pound, it was food for the mind and the spirit. At first, he remained quiet and attentive. From Yeats, for instance, he wanted to learn. Only slowly did he begin to insert tidbits of his quite formidable knowledge into the conversation and to pepper it with his wit and his extremely sharp critical faculties. Later, when he had become a permanent guest at Yeats's Monday evenings, he dominated the conversation. He soon founded his own club, "The Poets' Club," which met Wednesday evenings in the Eiffel Tower Restaurant on Percy Street.

During this time, he was writing poems for a new book, and this book, his third, accomplished what all the good connections never could have accomplished alone; it established Pound's place in the world of literature.

Pound had sent the manuscript to Elkin Mathews, the publisher of Oscar Wilde, Yeats, and the well-known "Yellow Book Series." Thereupon, he received a letter asking him to come to the rooms of the publishing house. Mathews told him he had read the poems, liked them, and wanted to print them. But he was of the opinion that such a risky venture on behalf of a completely unknown poet must to some extent be financially supported by that poet himself. Pound answered that he was of the same opinion and offered Mathews half of his current financial estate. He took a two-shilling piece from his pocket, and laying it on Mathews' desk, declared, that was all the money he had to his name.

Mathews printed *Personae*. It was published on

April 10, 1909, comprised fifty-nine pages, and immediately and strongly impressed London's literary
critics. Said *The Bookman,* "No new book of poems
for years had contained such a freshness of inspiration, such a strongly individual note, or been more
alive with indubitable promise." *The Observer* ad-
vised everyone who thought he could recognize real
poetry when he saw it to buy this book and keep it.
The *Daily Chronicle* spoke of the "old miracle that
cannot be defined, nothing more than a subtle entanglement of words, so that they rise out of their
graves and sing." But by far the best and most important review was written by Edward Thomas, certainly an influential man, for *The English Review.*

> To say what this poet has not is not difficult . . . He has no
> obvious grace, no sweetness, hardly any of the superficial good
> qualities of modern versifiers; not the smooth regularity of the
> Tennysonian tradition, nor the wavering, uncertain languor of
> the new, though there is more in his rhythms than is apparent at
> first through his carelessness of ordinary effects. He has not the
> current melancholy or resignation or unwillingness to live; nor
> the kind of feeling for nature that runs to minute description and
> decorative metaphor . . . full of personality and with such
> power to express it, that from the first to the last lines of most of
> his poems he holds us steadily in his own pure, grave, passionate
> world."[8]

Upon the appearance of *Personae,* Pound was suddenly a recognized poet of rank. He was twenty-four
years old. He had come to London with no letters of
recommendation, with no introductions, with no connections, and with three pounds in his pocket. But his
energy and his ability spoke for themselves.

What kinds of poems are in *Personae?* Some of
them had already appeared in *A Lume Spento* and
*Quinzaine,* for example, "In Durance" and "Sestina
Altaforte." The majority of the others are, in diction
and style, new studies in the manner of the trouba-

dours. "Cino" is the song of a minstrel on "the open road" in the "Italian Campagna 1309." It begins,

> Bah! I have sung women in three cities,
> But it is all the same;
> And I will sing of the sun.

"Na Audiart" is, as the note preceding it acknowledges, the song that Bertran of Born wrote in his despair at being refused the love of My Lady Maent of Montaignac. In the song, he begs of the several other ladies he names some trait of character or of body that each possesses to perfection, so that, putting them together, he may at last have some semblance of the perfection of the lady who has rejected him, the "ideal woman."

"Marvoil" is Pound's poetic version of the love lamentation of Arnaut de Marieuil. "Pierre Vidal Old" is a balladesque love song. There are poems in *Personae* for whose origins we must go back to Dante, or to the Latin of Propertius, or to the Italian Leopardi, or to the Frenchman Joachim du Bellay. Robert Browning and A. E. Housman are taken up as well. The sources are given in each case.

Pound is nowhere concerned about being "original" in his source of inspiration; quite the contrary, he is making the attempt to achieve a spontaneity of expression that bridges the lapse of time between the Middle Ages and the modern age. He is striving to bring the emotion of the original poet, his suffering, his passion, his character, directly to the heart of the modern reader, while at the same time, in manner of speech and in the spirit of the whole, remaining true to the epoch and the personality of the original. In this attempt, Pound admirably succeeds.

In other poems of *Personae,* Pound speaks for himself. The speaker in "Famam Librosque Cano" is a poet who is reflecting on his reading public and his fame. The diction oscillates between the romantic tone, which rather dominates, and a kind of colloquial speech that had seldom found entry into verse up to this time. This phenomenon is more obvious in the very few lines of "On Seeing His Own Face in a Glass." The natural diction of the first line, "O strange face there in the glass!" gives way to the archaic "ribald" in the very next line, "O ribald company, O saintly host"; two lines down, Pound reverts to his "ye," and the poem ends with the poet addressing his face in the mirror as "ye," an inner self out of another, older era.

In *Personae,* Pound has halted just before the breakthrough to modern poetic speech. His excellent ear for the musical cadence of language and his love for the verse of the Provençal poets were still hindrances on his way to creating a new "colloquial" language for verse, a language that does not lose its innate poetic melody and cadence simply because it makes use of everyday conversational expressions.

Pound had already begun to work at a theoretical basis for modern poetic diction. He had, above all, the "precise word" in mind, regardless of the social stratum of its origin, regardless even of the language of its origin, whether foreign or English—a preciseness of expression of which a corresponding exactness of rhythm must be an integral part.

*Personae* represents at one and the same time a turning point in lyrical practice that makes it a direct forerunner of modern poetry, as we know it today, and a stepping stone for Pound himself on his way toward a poetic language of his own. The Pound scholar Hugh Kenner maintains that these early poems are "poses," and it is certain that we can see the figures in *Personae* as actors in a drama in the antique manner, that is as

masked players of various roles. Pound himself described what he was after in a letter to William Carlos
Williams,

To me the short so-called dramatic lyric—at any rate the sort of
thing I do—is the poetic part of a drama the rest of which (to
me the prose part) is left to the reader's imagination or implied
or set in a short note. I catch the character I happen to be interested in at the moment he interests me, usually the moment of
song, self-analysis, or sudden understanding or revelation. And the
rest of the play would bore me and presumably the reader. I
paint my man as I *conceive* him. Et voilà tout![9]

Pound is at this point (1908) concerned with the
elimination of prose or nonlyrical passages and the
presentation exclusively of the essential moment. The
effect of such experimentation is not yet fully to be
felt in *Personae*. It has been noted that in this book
Pound saw the necessity of even including explanatory
notes with historical or biographical data to facilitate
the understanding of his verses.

But by the time his book of poems *Ripostes* was
printed in 1912, he was ready not only to leave such
information out but also to present a succession of
such essential "moments" within one poem without
any verbal indication of the connection between them.
He goes even beyond that to letting a juxtaposition of
two or more such moments stand for a meaning that
the reader must discover for himself.

It is this lack of explanatory or connecting matter, this saying something through something left un-
said, that makes Pound's later work so difficult to com-
prehend. The measure by which Pound approaches his
reader through use of a "living, spoken language" and
of the "precise word" is the same measure by which he
moves farther away from that reader's comprehension
through his omission of causal, binding, or comment-
ing thoughts.

What were the steps in Pound's development in
the four years between *Personae* and *Ripostes?* The
steps that an ingenious experimenter took to become
the first modern poet in English?

Pound describes those steps in 1914, well after the
completion of the process, as follows:

In the "search for oneself," in the search for "sincere self-expres-
sion," one gropes, one finds some seeming verity. One says "I am"
this, that, or the other, and with the words scarcely uttered one
ceases to be that thing.

I began this search for the real in a book called *Personae,* casting
off as it were, complete masks of the self in each poem. I continued in a long series of translations, which were but more
elaborate masks.[10]

We can follow Pound's road only by way of his
publications. In *Exultations,* which Mathews published at the end of 1909 upon the success of *Personae,* Pound is still largely the actor, the player who
expresses the objective reality of another. The "self"
to which Pound is finding his way is his artistic self.
It is not only nonpersonal and objective, it is deliberately stripped of the personal and the subjective.
Pound as an artist negates his subjective self and allows an objective self he has created to experience
reality. The exercises with which he was able to arrive
at this ascetic height were his translations. He thought
of them as the direct expression of another experienc-
ing self with whom he had identified himself for the
duration of his work on the translation.

Pound interrupted his work to return to the
United States for a visit in 1910. At this time, he was
famous in literary London and well-known in literary
America. He visited William Carlos Williams (who
the year before had traveled to London to see him),
spent a good deal of time in his home town of Wyncote, and lived in New York. He saw his country with

different eyes now, and his sojourn there left a strong impression. He asked himself whether New York was not the most beautiful city in the world, for "beside it Venice seemed like a tawdry scene in a playhouse." He described with passionate enthusiasm the life and the strength that were everywhere apparent to him in the book he next wrote upon his return to London, *Patria Mia*.[11] For all this, London remained his cultural home. The years from 1911 to 1920, which he spent there, are without a doubt the most important years in Pound's development as a poet.

In July 1911, Mathews printed still another small book of Pound's poems, *Canzoni*. Far from pointing the way toward *Ripostes*, however, in which poems of lasting quality appear, the first modern poems by Ezra Pound, some of the verses in *Canzoni* were later rejected by Pound himself and never reprinted. Pound said they "contained many false starts."[12]

In November of the same year, Pound's translation of the Anglo-Saxon poem "The Seafarer" appeared in the magazine *New Age*. It is not a false start but a decisive step in Pound's search for the "new" language that he had, to a great extent, found when he wrote *Ripostes*. The diction of the Anglo-Saxon poetry from which Pound profited is hard and clear. The verb and the noun dominate; adjectives are seldom used. The Anglo-Saxon language built new nouns not by borrowing from another language as modern English has borrowed from Latin, Scandinavian, and French (again Latin, but for the sake of conciseness, let us call it French since that was its immediate source); instead, two nouns that already existed were combined to build a new one. (German has retained this form of vocabulary enrichment.) For this reason, the Anglo-Saxon word immediately calls the "thing" to mind to which it refers, the word is an image of the thing.

"Tablecloth" or "armchair" are words that are built in this manner.

In contrast to this kind of language, the highly adjectival romanticizing English of the poems of Pound's contemporaries was abstract and vague. Anglo-Saxon poets again are adept at using strong sound elements based on an alliterative line with four heavily stressed syllables beginning in the same letter or letter combination. Pound retained this style element in his translation.

> Bitter breast-cares have I abided,
> Known on my keel many a care's hold . . .

It is of kindred spirit with Pound's own leaning toward a strong and word-bound cadence. Through his work with Anglo-Saxon poetry, Pound came to know the original technical possibilities of his own tongue in forming precise and vigorous word pictures. Later, he called such pictures "images." It is probably safe to say that the Anglo-Saxon translations, more than any others up to this point, were the decisive, formative step toward Pound's new language.

The writing of prose, however, was also an exercise in casting off the old in order to find his artistic self. In critical works such as *The Spirit of Romance,* published in 1910, Pound set about evaluating analytically the work of those authors whom he had up to now appreciated subjectively as artists: Lope de Vega, the troubadours, and the Romance authors of the Middle Ages in general; they had been the subject of his lectures at Polytechnic now for two years.

*The Spirit of Romance,* like all of Pound's prose, has been rather diversely criticized. Those who expected to find a scholarly study quite rightly found fault with the inadequate method of inquiry, with the large number of undocumented assertions, with the apparent unsoundness of arguments and theories advanced by Pound as though they were axiomatic. One Pound critic, George Dekker, for example, calls the work an enthusiastic vulgarization. Pound, he says, never got beyond the stage of an apprentice in Romance studies.[13] But in the introduction to the book, Pound himself had set up other than scholarly goals.

This book is not a philological work. Only by courtesy can it be said to be a study in comparative literature.

I am interested in poetry. I have attempted to examine certain forces, elements or qualities which were potent in the medieval literature of the Latin tongues, and are, I believe, still potent in our own. . . .

There is no attempt at historical completeness.[14]

Following this design, the work should be viewed rather as a documentation of Pound's thinking on these subjects than as an inquiry into the history of a literary epoch. It renders us numerous theses that point immediately to the imagist movement that Pound at this time called into being.

Pound does not himself accept the title of founding father of the imagists. He says the basic ideas on which this movement, which mobilized latent energies in English poetry, was founded must be ascribed to T. E. Hulme. In 1908, Hulme had established a "club" that met at the Eiffel Tower restaurant and had dominated that club for a year. Pound had been brought there by the actress Florence Farr. Hulme was impressed with the young American, and the admiration was mutual. A friendship grew of it that was quite fruitful for Pound. Hulme was a discerning observer and keen thinker and helped Pound achieve more preciseness of thought and expression. He seems to have been somewhat of a Dr. Samuel Johnson figure who is more effective in his conversation than in his writing.

The few poems that he left us (he was killed in
World War I) were published in Pound's book *Ripostes*
and later in more comprehensive collections of Pound's
poems.

The group that then called itself "The Imagists"
came from the older Hulme club, but Hulme himself
was no longer among them. Richard Aldington, who at
that time was in London with H. D. (Hilda Doolittle)
gives a quaint version of the birth of the movement.

Like other American expatriates Ezra and H.D. developed an almost insane relish for afternoon tea . . . they insisted on going to
the most fashionable and expensive tea-shops . . . Thus it came
about that most of our meetings took place in the rather prissy
milieu of some infernal bun-shop full of English spinsters. However, an extremely good time was had by all and we laughed
until we ached—at what I haven't the slightest recollection. . . .
Naturally then, the Imagist mouvemong was born in a tea-shop—
in the Royal Borough of Kensington. For some time Ezra had
been butting in on our studies and poetical productions, with
alternate encouragement and the reverse, according to his mood.
H.D. produced some poems, which I thought excellent, and she
either handed them or mailed them to Ezra. Presently each of us
received a ukase to attend the Kensington bun-shop. Ezra was
so worked up by these poems of H.D.'s that he removed his
pince-nez and informed us that we were Imagists. Was that the
first time I heard that Pickwickian word? I don't remember. According to the record, Ezra swiped the word from the English
philosopher T. E. Hulme. . . .

My own belief is that the name took Ezra's fancy, and that he
kept it in petto for the right occasion. If there were no Imagists,
obviously they would have to be invented. Whenever Ezra has
launched a new movement—and he had made such a hobby of it
that I always expect to find one day that Pound and Mussolini
are really one and the same person—he has never had any difficulty about finding members. He just calls on his friends.[15]

Aldington's conjecture is altogether believable.
But Pound was very much in earnest about the ideas
that were basic to this movement. He thought he recognized in H. D.'s verses the apt utilization of those

very principles which he himself had been working toward and that he had found to be realizable as he translated from the Anglo-Saxon. He called "The Seafarer" an imagist poem. He found imagist elements in Catullus's "Collis o Heliconii" and in the French poem "Charles d'Orleans." And he reasoned that imagism was fundamental to all English verse, as the language was made up of these three tongues, Anglo-Saxon, French, and Latin.

Imagism, therefore, had existed for a very long time, a type of poetry, said Pound, "where painting or sculpture seems as if it were 'just coming over into speech'." "Imagisme . . . has been known chiefly as a stylistic movement, as a movement of criticism rather than of creation."[16] Perhaps the clearest statement of the objectives of imagism is to be found in an article entitled "A Few Don'ts by an Imagist" which appeared shortly after the afternoon Aldington describes, in *Poetry,* a magazine that had not long before appeared for the first time in Chicago. The exact wording here has been reprinted in other articles about the movement that Pound published later and, we can therefore deduce, retained his approval. The imagists, he says, agreed on three rules for poetry:

I. Direct treatment of the "thing," whether subjective or objective.
II. To use absolutely no word which did not contribute to the presentation.
III. As regarding rhythm: to compose in sequence of the musical phrase, not in sequence of a metronome.[17]

Whether or not such rules are meaningful at all, whether or not they are "new" or applicable or have been applied, whether or not they are rather meaningless or even contrary to the aspirations of every sort of literature, are questions that become irrelevant in the face of the impact these publications had. Imagism became the most dynamic single force in modern English and American poetry.

The months during which Pound worked out the imagist theories were full of stimulation. The source of the major impulses was undoubtedly Yeats, who at this time was setting some of his own poems to music with friends. The compositions were recited publicly by Florence Farr. This type of melodic recital of verse fit in well with Pound's ideas about the natural cadence and melody of poetic language and enhanced his theories on the subject. Yeats introduced Pound beyond that into the realms of Neo-Platonic thought, of spiritistic interpretation of heathen mystery cults, and of Oriental philosophy. All of these found expression in Pound's work.

In late summer of 1912, Ezra Pound received a letter from Harriet Monroe, the editor of *Poetry* magazine, asking him if he wished to contribute to the publication. She wanted to publish the work of young poets. The letter that Pound wrote in answer represents his goals and endeavors as he saw them at that time. It is significant as well for his quickness and firmness of resolution and for the vigor with which he undertook a task he considered good and made it his own.

There is no other magazine in America which is not an insult to the serious artist and to the dignity of his art.

But? Can you teach the American poet that poetry *is* an *art,* an art with a technique, with media, an art that must be in constant flux, a constant change of manner, if it is to live? . . . Anyhow you have work before you . . .

—You may announce, if it's any good to you, that for the present such of my work as appears in America (barring my own books) will appear exclusively in your magazine. . . .

Are you for American poetry or for poetry? The latter is more important . . . The glory of any nation is to produce art that can be exported without disgrace to its origin. . . .

Anyhow I hope your ensign is not "more poetry"! but more interesting poetry and *maestria!*

If I can be of any use in keeping you or the magazine in touch with whatever is most dynamic in artistic thought, either here or in Paris—as much of it comes to me, and I *do* see nearly everyone that matters—I shall be glad to do so.

I send you all that I have on my desk . . .

P.S. Any agonizing that tends to hurry what I believe in the end to be inevitable, our American Risorgimento, is dear to me. That awakening will make the Italian Renaissance look like a tempest in a teapot! The force we have, and the impulse, but the guiding sense, the discrimination in applying the force, we must wait and strive for.[18]

Pound kept his word. He sent Harriet Monroe the work of the best writers of poetry and prose. He included the work of his friends, if he found it good, but also the work of men with whom he could establish little or no contact, such as D. H. Lawrence, whenever he found it to be of literary quality. Of course, it was not always easy to convince Miss Monroe that it was literature of quality that he sent in each case. She could not rise above her Puritan point of view. Some of the manuscripts she sent back as being too bold, others as even unseemly or improper. Pound didn't lose patience. His numerous letters to her make up what one might call a primer on the literary arts. It took him six months of intensive correspondence to induce her to print T. S. Eliot.

Naturally, Pound's work for the magazine was not completely altruistic. In part, he saw in Harriet Monroe a means to his own ends. Through her he had a literary outlet in the U.S. *Poetry* was the first in a long line of similar little magazines that owe Ezra Pound their profile if not their reputation. The editors of *A History of American Poetry,* Horace Gregory and Marya Zaturensky, maintain that Pound's influence can be traced through the files of at least fifty such magazines in Europe and the U.S. from 1916–1939.

Perhaps the best known of Pound's imagist poems is *"In a Station of the Metro,"* which appeared in his next book, *Lustra,* in 1915. It is a two-line poem which, according to Pound, it took him over a year to write. He describes the process in an article entitled "How I Began."

For well over a year I had been trying to make a poem of a very beautiful thing that befell me in the Paris underground. I got out of a train at La Concorde and in the jostle I saw a beautiful face, and then, turning suddenly, another and another, and then a beautiful child's face, and then another beautiful face. All that day I tried to find words for what this made me feel. That night as I went home along the rue Raynouard I was still trying. I could get nothing but spots of colour. I remember thinking that if I had been a painter I might have started a wholly new school of painting. I tried to write the poem weeks afterward in Italy, but found it useless. Then only the other night, wondering how I should tell the adventure, it struck me that in Japan, where a work of art is not estimated by its acreage and where sixteen syllables are counted enough for a poem if you arrange and punctuate them properly, one might make a very little poem which would be translated about as follows:

> The apparition of these faces in the crowd:
> Petals on a wet, black bough.

And there, or in some other very old, very quiet civilization, some one else might understand the significance.[19]

What Pound means by perfect harmony of image, rhythm, and sense can be seen in this short poem. The first line is dominated by the repetition of the long, dark vowels, "a" and "o," and soft word endings that allow the words to glide over into one another in a manner suggestive of the moving crowd in a Metro station. The word "petals" bursts into the tone picture by the very quality of its initial labial consonant and its short, hard syllables; the effect is underscored by the rhyming stop word "wet." These are two emphatic interruptions in the long-vowel run of the second line that remains in assonance to that of the first. The poem ends with two alliterated stresses that remind us of Anglo-Saxon poetry, a drum-beat of an ending, but the "ough" is a fading-out sound like that of the endlessly running Metro trains leaving the station.

The word that in tone-quality, placement in the poem, and rhythmic stress is the most accentuated, the central word, is "petals," and this word is the "image" in this imagist poem. It represents at once the appearance of the faces and the perception of the observer. Pound deliberately avoids a simile, "faces like petals," or a metaphor, "faces are petals" and leaves us only the apposition of "apparition" and "petals" so that we, in reading the poem, directly experience the moment of perception that the poet wants us to.

The poem, instead of telling of or describing an experience, is itself the experience. Pound describes the process. "An 'Image' is that which presents an intellectual and emotional complex in an instant of time," he says in his memoir on Gaudier-Brzeska.[20]

The 'one-image poem' is a form of super-position, that is to say, it is one idea set on top of another . . . In a poem of this sort one is trying to record the precise instant when a thing outward and objective transforms itself or darts into a thing inward and subjective.[21]

He compares this procedure of conciousness with similar processes that have been observed in impressionist painting.

It goes without saying that most of Pound's imagist poems are longer than the one just considered. The image is then expanded or it is presented in a series of partial moments of perception that cast reflection in their turn like the facets of a precious stone.

However, very few imagist poems reach the degree of consummation that distinguishes the one above.

A whole row of contemporary poets tried their hand at imagist verse; H. D. is the only one who can be said to have both remained true to the stated imagist principles and to have maintained a high standard in her art.

The American poet Amy Lowell soon identified herself with the imagist group and wrote a few good poems as well as a large number of bad ones. She emphasized the poet's freedom from traditional poetic forms, a freedom that had originally been regarded by the imagists as a means toward unity of form and meaning. Miss Lowell, however, neglected the other imagist principles and became, in effect, a crusader for free verse.

In 1914, Pound edited the first anthology of imagist poetry. Soon afterward, he began to see how the most excellent characteristics of the imagist method were being forced into the background by Amy Lowell and the other free-verse poets. When Pound read the contributions Amy Lowell had collected for the second anthology, he withdrew from the enterprise, saying that their literary quality was equal to zero. Amy Lowell thereupon published some rather angry letters in an attempt to discredit Pound. He was certainly equal to answering in kind and in the end demanded that the word "Imagist" be deleted from the title of the anthology. Amy Lowell refused to honor any such demand. In the following three years, Miss Lowell edited three successive volumes of the anthology *Some Imagist Poets.* Pound called these poets "Amygists," and time has shown that his judgment of their literary quality was sound. At any rate, the whole affair was good publicity.

In the meantime, Pound had become acquainted

with two other women who frequented the circle around Yeats. One was Dorothy Shakespear, the daughter of the Olivia Shakespear whose name has become known as a long-time correspondent of Yeats.

It is typical of Pound that, in the first two years of his friendship with Dorothy, he seldom ever spoke or wrote about her. William Carlos Williams says that there was always a picture of a woman and a candle next to it on Pound's desk, but Pound never said whose likeness it was. They were married in 1914.

Dorothy Shakespear was a musically talented and intelligent young woman who had been brought up in a refined family. She was reserved, ladylike, and tactful.

The second woman was Harriet Weaver, who financed a small suffragette magazine, *The New Freewoman*. She frequented the Hulme group and soon became a willing victim of Pound's eloquence. He convinced her that her magazine needed a literary section and that he could deliver one. After a few issues with his literary section had appeared, he even persuaded her to change the name of the magazine. On January 1, 1914, it appeared for the first time as *The Egoist*.

Pound seems to have been drawn to (unmarried) literarily active women. The next one was Margaret Anderson, editor of the magaine *The Little Review*. These women, late products of the bluestocking movement, served Pound over shorter or longer periods of time as a means by which he could accomplish his literary aims. It was important to him to have at hand various organs of publication for experiments, critical observations, translations, and poems. One could as little remain in the limelight of the world of letters as develop one's own poetic capabilities by writing and publishing only books of poems or prose at longer intervals. Still and all, Pound's connections to such women could not and did not remain peaceful.

The most sensational and shortest lived of Pound's little magazines was *BLAST*. The first of two issues appeared on April 20, 1914. The size of a telephone directory, and printed on coarse yellow paper, it threatened in huge black letters destruction and ruin to all those forces that had led up to 1914. Aristocracy and proletarianism, Victorianism, Rousseauism, the bourgeoisie, sentimentality, even rhyme and form, museums and art—everything must be blasted up in smoke. *BLAST* hit London like dynamite. A new Pound movement had come into being, his own version of futurism, and he called it "vortex." Vortex, he said, is the point of highest energy. In mechanics, it represents the point of maximum effectiveness.

Pound drummed the "vorticists" together after the imagist movement had died for him. Hulme was again the central figure. Other members were Wyndham Lewis, the English painter and novelist, Jacob Epstein, Arnold Dolmetsch, and Henri Gaudier-Brzeska, a young sculptor with whose work Pound was enraptured. The group introduced itself first in *The Egoist*, but the profile of this magazine was already set. *BLAST* brought about the sensation that suited the vorticists. They met in "The Cave of the Golden Calf," which Pound called London's first night club. The proprietress was Frieda, the third wife of August Strindberg.

*BLAST* has been variously evaluated. Some saw it as merely blown-up emptiness. But especially Gaudier's contributions on the theory of art were elucidating and forward-looking. When the second issue appeared a year later, the young sculptor—twenty-three years old —had fallen in France. Shortly after, the group broke up.

At the outbreak of World War I, the years of the "masks" had ended for Pound. He had attained undisputed poetic rank with the publication of *Ripostes*. The imagist and vorticist movements had had formidable impact on contemporary letters. In Ford Madox Ford and Elkin Mathews, he had found publishers who were his loyal supporters. He had in a series of little magazines a constant outlet for his work. The most recognized artists in London held both his poetry and his opinions in esteem, and he could reckon them among his friends.

In the U. S., he was, as the critic Mullins puts it, "a legendary figure."[22] The American poet Carl Sandburg wrote in 1915, "If I were driven to name one individual who, in the English language, by means of his own example of creative art in poetry, has done most of living men to incite new impulses in poetry, the chances are I would name Ezra Pound."[23]

Pound had within six years created this position for himself in the world of English and American literature. He was now twenty-nine years old.

# 4

*Il Miglior Fabbro*

Pound's influence on the work of his time and on the propagation of the best of this work is unmistakable. The first of the poets on whom he was to have an impact was William Butler Yeats. Pound had chosen London as his place of residence in order to meet him. At the time, the Irishman was almost fifty years old. His collected works in eight volumes had been printed (1908), so that his reputation was established. It would seem that he had reached the culmination of his poetic career, his most important works having been written, printed, and recognized as such.

It has already been pointed out that Yeats played a significant role for Pound in his first London years, ushering him into the literary society of the city as well as stimulating him to study new fields of thought. The influence of Yeats's poetry on Pound's early work is considerable, but it was of relatively short duration. Pound began very soon to go his own way. There was no longer any place in verse for "beautiful phrases," for rhetoric, for sonorous, meaningless adjectives, for images with "hazy edges," for the combination of a concrete epithet and an abstract idea ("blue truth"), or the reverse. The era of precision had begun, and the arts, too, must pay it tribute.

Yeats had neither closed his mind to change and innovation, nor was his sensitivity to the sound of good poetry dulled. Pound's knowledge and his verse had impressed Yeats, and he began to experiment in the manner of the principles and theories by which Pound worked. During the winter of 1913 and the following two winters, Pound functioned as Yeats's personal secretary. In a letter to Lady Gregory, the Irish folklore authoress, Yeats comments on their relationship,

the criticism I got from them [Pound and Sturge Moore] has given me new life and I have made that Tara poem a new thing and am writing with new confidence having got Milton off my back. Ezra is the best critic of the two. He is full of the middle ages and helps me to get back to the definite and concrete, away from modern abstractions. To talk over a poem with him is like getting you to put a sentence into dialect. All becomes clear and natural. Yet in his own work he is very uncertain, often very bad though very interesting sometimes. He spoils himself by too many experiments and has more sound principles than taste.[1]

Yeats began to write a new type of poetry from this time on. Ten years later, in 1923, he received the Nobel Prize for literature. It was, to go back, the second time that Pound had been instrumental in the choice of a Nobel Prize recipient. Together with Yeats, he had given considerable support to the candidature of the Indian poet Tagore, who was awarded the honor in 1913. Much later two other authors who benefited from working with Pound, T. S. Eliot, and Ernest Hemingway, also became Nobel Prize holders. Pound himself has never been honored in this or any comparable manner.

T. S. Eliot simply came to visit Pound one day in London in 1914. The young man from the state of Missouri brought poems along that he had been writing since 1911 and that no one had seen fit to print. Pound sent Eliot's "The Love-Song of J. Alfred Prufrock" to Harriet Monroe with the comment, "The most interesting contribution I've had from an American."[2] Miss Monroe, however, had misgivings. She found the conclusion of the poem too depressing. Pound bombarded her with letters and refused absolutely to ask Eliot to alter as much as one word. Instead, he reminded her that he had once already contemplated terminating his work with and for *Poetry* magazine. After half a year, in June 1915, he finally gained his stand and Eliot's "Lovesong" was printed in *Poetry*. It was the beginning of Eliot's poetic career.

During this time Pound had the feeling that the high standard of art that he wanted to see established was not attainable in London.

There is no organized or coordinated civilization left, only individual scattered survivors. . . . No use waiting for masses to develop a finer taste, they aren't moving that way. . . . Darkness and confusion as in Middle Ages; no chance of general order or justice; we can only release an individual here or there. . . . It is for us who want good work to provide means of its being done.[3]

This passage is taken from a letter of entreaty that Pound sent from Paris somewhat later to many friends and acquaintances whom he could trust to share his views on art, asking them for financial support to enable T. S. Eliot to work without pecuniary cares for at least one year. Not very much could be collected.

Pound did Eliot the better service by editing his long poem "The Waste Land," undoubtedly the most famous single poem of the twentieth century. Pound's help here is certainly the most meritorious of his many accomplishments as mentor to young talent, and Eliot has documented his debt to Pound whenever and wherever he could. He dedicated "The Waste Land" to Pound with the words "il miglior fabbro" (the better craftsman), which Dante had used in reference to Arnaut Daniel. Pound had cut the poem upon which Eliot's fame is based to one half of its original length and given critical comments that were indispensable toward bringing the work to its final form.

The correspondence between the two men during this work (Pound was already living in Paris) makes up a valuable document in literary history. Neither Ezra Pound the poet, who could himself have written this poem, nor T. S. Eliot was capable of the self-criticism that was necessary to bring it to culmination of form. When Eliot was once asked what advice he would give to apprentices at poetry, he said, read Pound. "There is in fact no one else to study."[4] In its laudation, however, the Nobel Prize jury called Eliot the epoch-making pioneer of modern poetry.

James Joyce was another of Pound's "discoveries" and protégés. Of *Chambermusic,* the small book of poems that Joyce published in 1908, no notice at all had been taken. Yeats had it, probably for the sake of its having been written by a fellow Irishman, and he passed it on to Pound, who, recognizing its merits, asked Joyce in 1913 for permission to reprint some of the poems in the anthology *Des Imagistes.*

Apart from the poems, Joyce sent him the first chapter of *A Portrait of the Artist as a Young Man,* and Pound began in 1914 to publish the chapters of this book as a series in *The Egoist.* The following summer, Pound's critique of Joyce's *The Dubliners* appeared in this magazine as well. It was the first published appreciation of Joyce's prose that can be taken seriously.

Through Pound's efforts, Joyce, who was in financial difficulty, also received some hundred English pounds from the Royal Literary Fund. And it was doubtless Pound again who gave the decisive impetus to Harriet Weaver's decision to set up a trust fund for Joyce that for some time gave him pecuniary independence and made it possible for him to receive medical treatment for his failing eyesight, to bear the costs of the long mental illness of his daughter, and to write the great novels *Ulysses* and *Finnegans Wake.*

It was Pound's wish and intention to publish *Ulysses* as a series in *The Egoist* as well, but no printer in London would declare himself willing to set the type. The printers found the novel indecent. Some short time before, Pound had seen an issue of the Chicago magazine *The Little Review,* which had con-

tained a number of blank pages. The editor, Margaret
Anderson, had offered the explanation that she could
find nothing that merited publication. Pound sent her
a letter saying he was looking for an official organ in
which T. S. Eliot, James Joyce, and Wyndham Lewis
could be published. *Ulysses* was then first printed in
*The Little Review* as a series over the next three
years.

Four of the issues in question were seized and
burned by the U.S. Post Office as being "obscene."
Margaret Anderson and her assistant Jane Heap were
arrested at the instigation of the American Society for
the Suppression of Vice and put into jail. The financial
benefiters of this witchhunt were the pirate presses
that reprinted *Ulysses* in the United States and, with
no royalties to the author, sold it at prices of one hundred to two hundred dollars a copy. Joyce was, now
as ever, living on donated money.

By no means, however, was Pound unreservedly
impressed with everything Joyce wrote. He had sharply
criticized some parts of *Ulysses* and could not see *Finnegans Wake* at all. He called it an "aimless search for
exaggeration. . . . I havnt patience to wade through
it/thank god I am not employed to estimate the
amount of real metal in low grade ores/(no pun in-
tended)."[5]

There are further examples of Pound's excursions
in the discovery and support of the most talented of
the moderns. A few are Robert Frost, D. H. Lawrence,
Jacob Epstein, and Wyndham Lewis. The number of
aspiring young authors who sought his aid was very
large, and if he found their work good, he answered.

Noel Stock, the Australian literary scholar, maintains that beyond any doubt it was Ezra Pound who
led English letters out of a state of stagnation. T. S.
Eliot affirms that, "He liked to be the impresario for

younger men, as well as the animator of artistic activity in any milieu in which he found himself.

In this role he would go to any length of generosity and kindness . . ."[6] Pound himself says, "My problem is to keep alive a certain group of advancing poets, to set arts in their rightful place as the acknowledged guide and lamp of civilization . . . Scholarship is but a hand-maid to the arts."[7]

It became clear to Pound during the years 1914–1915 what a decisive role art can play in the overall health of a culture. His thoughts in this direction were fostered by his study of certain manuscripts by Ernest Fenollosa, an American scholar in oriental culture, and by his inquiries into original works of Oriental philosophy. Pound had been introduced to the widow of Fenollosa by Yeats; their meeting was to have far-reaching consequences for Pound's poetry.

Mrs. Fenollosa saw in him the man she had been searching for to arrange and edit the many notes, manuscripts, and translations that her husband had left unpublished at his death. This work was Pound's introduction into the art of Japan and China and formed the basis for his future occupation with the ideogram as a literary style element.

That Pound should have grasped so readily at Fenollosa's ideas is characteristic of his manner of acquiring knowledge, which was more eclectic than systematic. He was only too ready to accept new ideas and facts that supported theories he had already formed on his own. Fenollosa's inquiries and conclusions were directly in line with Poundian thought on language since 1912. Language as the means for preserving thought, he said, was constantly being worn away, exhausted, and it was the function of writers, therefore, constantly to coin language anew. Strength and exactness of words—these were the guiding themes.

The most comprehensive statements Pound has made in this vein are contained in a book he wrote somewhat later (1931) called *How to Read.*

When . . . the application of word to thing goes rotten, i.e. becomes slushy and inexact, or excessive or bloated, the whole machinery of social and of individual thought and order goes to pot.[8]

Such thought processes came to fruition much later when Pound was translating and adapting for his own use the philosophy of Confucius. The fourth paragraph of Pound's final version of the Confucian *Ta Hio* reads as follows:

The men of old wanting to clarify and diffuse throughout the empire that light which comes from looking straight into the heart and then acting, first set up good government in their own states; wanting good government in their own states, they first established order in their own families; wanting order in the home, they first disciplined themselves; desiring self-discipline, they rectified their own hearts; and wanting to rectify their hearts, they sought precise verbal definitions of their inarticulate thoughts (the tones given off by the heart); wishing to obtain precise verbal definitions, they set to extend their knowledge to the utmost. The completion of knowledge is rooted in sorting things into organic categories.[9]

Hugh Kenner informs us that Pound has continually referred to this Confucian work as "what I believe" and comments further, "It is to this tradition, with its almost Confucian progression between empirical inquiry, linguistic sincerity, private worth and public benefit that Pound may be said to belong."[10]

The health of a society is only one result of maintaining this strict purity of word; it is the outward result. But there are inner consequences as well for "ching ming" (the purification of the word), an ideogram that in the original as well as in the English transliteration is often to be found in the *Cantos.* It can lead, for the poet who makes it his habit of thought, to an inner depth of immediate cognition that makes him perceptive to truths common to the thought and art of all cultures.

It was now that Pound began to conceive the idea of writing a long poem that would take up into its fabric the history of man and the multiplicity of his civilizations. He contented himself for the time being, however, with the publication of *Cathay* (April 1915), in which the first fruits of his Oriental studies appear. Pound wrote that these poems were, "For the most part from the Chinese of Rihaku, from the notes of the late Ernest Fenollosa, and the decipherings of the professors Mori and Ariga."[11]

It follows that Pound had sought the aid of experts in the Oriental languages for his translations, but it would be a serious misjudgment were we to conclude from that, that Pound now wished to render us exact linguistic translations any more than he had from the Provençal or the Latin heretofore.

The philologists found, as usual, a great deal of fault with *Cathay*; the poets, on the contrary, found a great deal to praise. T. S. Eliot, for instance, said, "Pound is the inventor of Chinese poetry for our time."[12] At any rate, Oriental forms of poetry are no longer uncommon in English and American letters, and this is, to some extent, thanks to Pound. Beyond that, it is doubtful whether he would, with philologically acceptable translations, have been able to convey to us the spirit and beauty of these poems that his renderings of them transmit.

What is peculiar to the Oriental short poem in the version given by Pound can be seen by the example of "Leave-Taking near Shoku." A scene or an incident is described briefly and is followed by an aphoristic comment on which the poem ends that at first glance seems to bear no causal or logical connection to the

scene described. The poem lives of the tension that is
set up by juxtaposing the experience to the thought,
but the reader must himself provide the link between
the two. This poetic method is in keeping with
Pound's basic ideas on the "dramatic short poem" that
presents in verse the dramatically essential moments of
an event or for a person and omits all transitional matter. Pound utilizes this method to an ever increasing
degree, and it becomes at last the basic element in the
construction of the *Cantos*.

Pound was engaged at this time in diverse activities, the very number of which would have staggered
the energies of another man. He served as editor of
two other books that were published in 1915: the poetic works of Lionel Johnson and the *Catholic Anthology*. He claims to have done the latter solely for
the satisfaction of seeing sixteen pages of T. S. Eliot
printed in succession. During the same year, he also
completed the necessary work on the manuscripts of
Fenollosa to prepare a book of Japanese noh plays for
press; arranged and edited a collection of letters from
the correspondence between Yeats and his father; reg-
ularly made monthly contributions to *Poetry, The
Little Review,* and *The Egoist,* and occasionally as
well to other magazines like the political journal *New
Age*.

This journal was published by Alfred Richard
Orage, a close friend of the Scottish engineer Major
C. H. Douglas, whose name is well known among
economists. Together, the two pursued in a half-dilet-
tante, half-scientific manner various studies in the related fields of history, politics, and economy.

Douglas, who is the founder of the "Social Credit"
movement, supported the theory that all the evil in
the world can be traced to fallacious economic policy.
The "real credit" of a nation, he maintained, rests in

the people themselves, and specifically in their power of production. There is, however, a perversion of this natural order and its source is the concentration of capital in the hands of a very few, which enables capital to control labor. These few hands, he said, belonged to Jews.

Douglas had various complex, and self-contradictory plans for the amelioration of the situation as he saw it, but he found for the present no listeners among economically schooled or politically interested people. He maintained of course that this was simply a part of the "Jewish plot." Later, around 1933, his ideas had enough resonance to win the "Social Credit" movement acknowledgment outside of England. Pound, at any rate, was convinced that Douglas's theories were sound.

Orage had begun as early as 1911 to publish articles by Pound in *New Age*. From 1917–1920, Pound wrote music and concert critiques for the journal under the pseudonym William Atheling. These critiques are proof of Pound's extensive knowledge in the field of music. Unfortunately, his knowledge of politics was not comparably extensive. Nor did his intuition in political questions make a good showing.

It was not long before he mixed political observations and commentary into his articles on literature and the arts. The question as to how it is possible that a man of such sure judgment in aesthetic matters should have so sadly failed to grasp the political scene can by no means be answered with a mere reference to his personal relationship to Orage and Douglas. The reasons are complex and profound.

World War I was a deep shock for Pound. Suddenly and violently, the arts were forced out of their central place in the cosmic order. Politics were now first in rank. Artists were compelled to first see to the order of political affairs so that they might be able to return to the arts.

That the major and basic evil of the time was an economic evil was for Pound and many others as good as axiomatic. To be sure, the artist produced goods for the nation like every other laborer, but the nation had no use for these goods.

Pound had, in 1914, in a review of a book by Allan Upward, stated, "A nation is civilized in so far as it recognizes the special faculties of the individual and makes use of them."[13] The artist must concern himself with "cold subjects" like economics in order to continue to exist.

Twenty years ago, before "one," "we," "the present writer" or his acquaintances began to think about "cold subjects like economics" one began to notice that the social order hated *any* art of maximum intensity and preferred dilutations. The best artists were unemployed, they were unemployed long before, or at any rate appreciably before, the unemployment crises began to make the front page of the newspapers.

Capitalist society, or whatever you choose to call the social organization of 1905 to 1915 was *not* getting the most out of its available artistic "plant."

"I give *myself* work" said Epstein when he was asked if he had any.

The best writers of my generation got into print or into books mainly via small organizations initiated for that purpose and in defiance of the established publishing business of their time. This is true of Joyce, Eliot, Wyndham Lewis and the present writer, from the moment his intention of breaking with the immediate past was apparent.[14]

Such were the difficulties that Pound experienced with the publication of his book *Lustra* in 1916. This book contained *Cathay,* several translations from the Chinese, and some new original poems, the greater number of which had already appeared in print in one or the other magazine without evoking much favorable notice from the critics.

When *Lustra* was to go into print, Pound's publisher Mathews became anxious that the book would offend the public and wanted to withdraw it and pay Pound a sum of twenty-five pounds as compensation. Pound protested.

Finally, two separate versions of *Lustra* were printed; one was a private edition of two hundred copies containing the complete and unaltered text; the second was sold to the public and was shorter by eight poems ("Salutation the Second," "Commission," "The New Cake of Soap," "Epitaph," "Meditatio," "Phyllidula," "The Patterns," and "The Seeing Eye"), all of which are relatively harmless. The next year they even appeared in the American edition that was put out by the New York publisher Alfred A. Knopf.

Knopf, too, however, made two separate versions of *Lustra*. This time the private edition of sixty copies contained one poem that was not included in the regular edition, but it was not one of the eight Mathews had left out. It was "The Temperament," which, read today, is anything but obscene and can only be thought to have fallen innocent victim to American prudery.

It was 1917. Pound's Byronesque airs were no longer new, no longer caused a stir, and had even begun to appear a bit silly. The war had sobered esoteric society. In the light of the long lists of the dead, it struck one as trivial to be collecting money for the support of needy authors. There were more serious concerns.

These seriously concerned Pound, too, and he wanted to take action. It was a part of his pioneer spirit, of his sense of mission, or his naïve Americanism, that he saw the necessity of *acting* to alter an unacceptable situation.

That he had fallen into the hands of Douglas and Orage was an unfortunate coincidence, but he had only to apply his principles about studying any given matter with absolute thoroughness, as he had, for instance, studied the troubadours, to discover the erroneous thinking in Douglas's system. This thoroughness was, however, a thing of the past. Instead, a trait of character revealed itself that with age became increasingly significant for Pound. He became inspired with a cause at the first superficial glance, and he acted. The more he was censured for his view, the more passionately did he hold to it.

Pound wrote increasingly numerous articles on political economics, but not with an increasingly broad basis in fact. Charles Norman, the Pound biographer, says, "Reading Pound on economics, one sometimes has the feeling that he is learning more about art, culture and Pound than he is about economics."[15]

The entanglement had effects in the other direction as well. There are passages in the *Cantos* that treat entirely of political economics. As Van O'Connor puts it, "Pound's economic theories, the flow of his radio talks and the blood of his Cantos, originate from the Social Credit plan of Major C. H. Douglas and the doctrine of 'free money' of Silvio Gesell."[16]

Pound had become acquainted with the thoughts of Silvio Gesell (1862–1930) through Douglas. The Swiss economic theorist had been, for a short time in 1919, Minister of Finance in the Munich Soviet Republic and was the author of the book *Natürliche Wirtschaftsordnung durch Freiland und Freigeld* [Natural Economic Order through Free Land and Free Money], which was published in 1911 and went into the ninth edition in 1951. (The association which he founded was forbidden in Germany under Hitler in 1933, refounded in 1945, and still has today some 2,600 members in western Germany.) Van O'Connor gives a clear and concise analysis of Gesell's doctrine:

Gesell wished to eliminate non-labor incomes, such as interest and rent. He proposed issuing "shrinking money" (*Schwundgeld*) which would weekly lose 1% of its face value, under a purchasing power control. Thus such money could not be withheld from the market; it would cease to draw primary interest and become free. Douglas blamed our poverty-in-the-midst-of-plenty and the boom-depression cycles on the control of production and credit by a few financiers. Let us, he said, form one great holding company of securities . . . , compute the total national wealth, and, upon this, declare all citizens a certain national dividend to be paid monthly. With the control of prices, wages, profits, with the consumer's demands parallel with production, the national dividend becomes the difference between production and consumption. Establish an equitable distribution of social credit; maintain private enterprise under a controlled profit system.[17]

Pound found in these theories his central theme for the *Cantos,* usury. The controllers of money, he says, appropriate too much power over the people. The people themselves have yet to understand the essence of money. They think of money as a commodity to be bought and sold at market instead of as what it really is: first, a means for the easier exchange of commodities; second, a measure of the relative value of commodities; and third, a form of security for the future exchange of commodities. Usurers take advantage of the ignorance of the people and pervert the original and true character of money to the benefit of themselves and the damage of the common good. The watchword was: Down with usury.

These were the ideas to which Pound dedicated himself in 1916 and 1917, the years that marked his growing dissatisfaction with his life in London. He felt hindered in his poetic development although he had already begun work on the first cantos. The long poem "Homage to Sextus Propertius," which he wrote during this time, mirrors his state of mind. It is one of the "translations" from the Latin peculiar to Ezra Pound. He maintained that there was a strong like-

ness between Latin and English literature. Poets like
Catullus and Propertius had "approximately the same
problems as we have. The metropolis, the imperial
posts to all corners of the known world."[18] "Homage,"
Pound said,

presents certain emotions as vital to me in 1917, faced with the
infinite and ineffable imbecility of the British Empire, as they
were to Propertius some centuries earlier, when faced with the
infinite and ineffable imbecility of the Roman Empire. These
emotions are defined largely, but not entirely, in Propertius' own
terms.[19]

"Homage" ran into the same storm of protest from
philologists that had formerly been loosed upon
Pound's Arnaut Daniel translations or his rendering
of Chinese verse in *Cathay*. It was not until 1947 that
a philologist of rank, Lawrence Richardson, clarified
convincingly for the philologically learned the indis-
putable merits of this work.

In the meantime, literary critics, reviewers, and
professors were engaged in an equally bitter controversy over "Homage." Robert Graves, for instance,
sought to give detailed scientific proof of Pound's errors and inefficiency in Latin translation. Dekker, on
the other hand, writes:

As for his translations I think that his most brilliant (perhaps
unrepeatable) solution was in "Homage to Sextus Propertius,"
where his "translation" is at its widest: only a food (or Robert
Graves) would regard it as a translation. . . . But it is clearly a
triumphant evasion of the problem, not even a near solution.[20]

In order to appreciate "Homage," one must read
it aloud. Among serious Pound critics, it was Stock
who best recognized that,

In "Propertius" Pound's music and his subject are very nearly
one. His technical resources were such by this time that they were
able to place, without embarrassment, any subject they happened
to encounter, no matter what turns, twists, changes of pace, or

modulations were necessary for its proper apprehension in verse. The poem may be said to have brought a new "music" into English, not a louder or bigger "music" exactly, but, if we turn to symphonic music for a rough parallel, some definite change as we find in the late symphonies of Mozart.[21]

"Homage to Sextus Propertius" was first printed in 1919 as a serial publication in *New Age*. It was then included in Pound's next book of poems *Quia Pauper Amavi*. At this time, Pound was setting up a draft of those cantos that have since become known as the "Hell Cantos" and that treat as a theme the Hell that was England; simultaneously, he was at work on the long poem "Hugh Selwyn Mauberley," which he described as his farewell to London. It was published in 1920. In 1921, Pound left England and never returned.

Various critics consider "Hugh Selwyn Mauberley" Pound's best poem, a high point in his works that he never again achieved. It is certainly true that Pound was at the peak of his technical ability and true as well that his departure from London, and therefore the poem that marks it, signified the end of a defined period in his development.

The biographical elements of the poem, which are not to be denied, should not seduce us into believing that the title figure is Ezra Pound. The poem has various elements in common with Eliot's "Lovesong," which Pound knew very well and by which it is possible, to a great extent, to identify Eliot with Prufrock.

However, Hugh Kenner is right in maintaining that Pound's relationship to Mauberley is more comparable to Joyce's relationship to Stephen Daedalus in *Portrait of the Artist*. Mauberly is not the artist himself, but a parody of the artist. The poem reflects the rich harvest in style and technique that Pound had gathered over the last fifteen years. It concentrates on the impressions that literary life in postwar England had made on a sensitive observer.

Pound maintains the point of view of the observer throughout the poem; instead of the former pose or mask, he wears his true character, that of the objective viewer. There is no trace of passion or sentiment. Pound is writing from the critical distance that his complete control of his medium and himself has afforded him. He controls, therefore, the reader as well.

Upon reading "Hugh Selwyn Mauberley," the critics were ready to negate Pound's entire development and the essential quality of his verse up to that point in order to avoid seeing the sharply ironic aspects of the poem, which threatened in its criticism the very basis of literary critique as practiced. Instead, they were happy to remark that Pound had learned from Eliot something completely new and applied it, that here was a poem full of real feeling in which the poet concedes his failure in society.

Pound's irony is of the uttermost subtlety and it conceals his profound bitterness, but it should not have been that difficult for critics of poetry to discover. The bitterness of tone is apparent when Pound lists the "ideals" for which soldiers sacrificed their lives. He confronts political slogans with naked truths. His social vignettes are pitiless.

It is nonsense to speak of the "Brennbaum" vignette as anti-Semitic. The name is probably to be associated with Max Beerbohm. At any rate, the eight lines are a parody on the "cult of style" in London literary circles. One might as well contend that the tenth episode is anti-Yeats. Seen on the whole, the poem is a masterpiece of satirical verse. But London's reviewers were deaf to Pound's language.

Ezra Pound's years in London ended with a sensation. A certain Lascelles Abercrombie, who wrote for the *Times Literary Supplement* and whom Pound found abominable, had during the war published sentimental patriotic verses. When an article about the "high art" of Milton by Abercrombie appeared, it was the decisive provocation for Pound. He wrote Abercrombie that his stupidity represented a menace to the public and challenged him to a duel.

Some Pound biographers have it that Abercrombie regarded the letter with humor and suggested that the dueling weapons be the unsold books of both parties used as throwing missiles. Others say he came to Yeats for advice, but fled when it was Pound who opened the door to Yeats's rooms. Ford Madox Ford's version is that he himself convinced Abercrombie that Pound was an excellent swordsman, whereupon Abercrombie, completely forgetting in his fear that the challenged party had the choice of weapons, immediately ran to Scotland Yard, and that the police urged Pound to leave the country.

Pound arrived in Paris early in 1921.

# 5

## The
## Minstrel

$E$zra Pound went traveling. It is tempting to think of him as one of the medieval wandering gleemen. T. S. Eliot had, during Pound's London years, already noticed a certain nervous energy peculiar to Pound and remarked:

> he seemed always to be only a temporary squatter. This appearance was due, not only to his restless energy—in which it was difficult to distinguish the energy from the restlessness and fidgets, so that every room, even a big one, seemed too small for him—but to a kind of resistance against growing into any environment. In America, he would no doubt have always seemed on the point of going abroad; in London, he always seemed on the point of crossing the Channel. I have never known a man, of any nationality, to live so long out of his native country without seeming to settle anywhere else.[1]

It was an impossibility for an artist of American birth to acclimatize himself fully to Paris in the 1920s. The main reason was that a whole colony of American artists lived there at that time, and they formed a tight clique. Their nonconformity was their most distinguishing characteristic. Pound blew in among them, the epitome of a Bohemian, in a flowing cape of extravagant dimensions, his red beard cut to an even sharper point than before, his lion's mane wild. Pound was enjoying the fresh Parisian breeze.

The central figure among the American expatriates in Paris was Gertrude Stein, the poetess to whom the now-famous sentence is ascribed, "You are all the lost generation." Hemingway chose this dictum as his motto for the novel *The Sun Also Rises*. It aptly characterizes what was the most talented generation of artists in the history of America.

Gertrude Stein undoubtedly saw Pound as a potential threat to her pre-eminent position in Parisian literary life. Perhaps she perceived, too, that he didn't belong to the "lost," at any rate, not to the rank and file. There was no mistaking the quick assumption of leadership that was characteristic of him. The result was that Pound was only twice present in Gertrude Stein's rooms. She found him interesting, but not amusing. He said the exact opposite of her. Stein adherents were soon to be found in the rooms of Ezra Pound, but Pound was interested neither in a feud with her nor in forming any new literary clique. Instead, he was looking for young talent.

He rented a first-floor studio (address: Notre Dame des Champs) where Whistler, whom he deemed the greatest American painter, had lived before him. He met Hemingway, F. Scott Fitzgerald, E. E. Cummings, and Henry Miller. His old friends T. S. Eliot, Wyndham Lewis, Ford Madox Ford, Richard Aldington, all lived in Paris for shorter or longer periods of time during Pound's four-year stay there. Here, Pound met James Joyce for the first time after years of correspondence. New acquaintances joined the number, the most conspicuous of whom was probably Tristan Tzara, the "father" of Dadaism. Pound also became acquainted with Georges Braque, Jean Cocteau, Constantin Brancusi, and George Antheil.

Pound began to take novel steps in his musical endeavors, which had begun in London in 1920 when he collaborated with the composer Agnes Bedford on a small study of five troubadour songs. The book was an attempt to reproduce the art of the troubadours, including their notes and text, in a manner meaningful for the twentieth century. Some degree of compositional skill, therefore, was indispensable to such a task. Pound learned a great deal from Agnes Bedford, and now he set about composing an opera using some songs by François Villon.

When the opera was finished, Pound invited the singer Yves Tinayre to tea. The tea table was a pack-

ing box covered with a tablecloth. Dorothy Pound
served the tea with a perfection of social grace and
then passed the one available spoon around.

Tinayre was impressed with Pound's idea and
the execution of the libretto, Villon's ballads, the
music, the novel instrumentation with a few trom-
bones, and the troubadour character of the songs.
Pound himself sang, although he couldn't carry a tune.

Whenever Tinayre related this episode, even
years later, he could hardly speak for laughing. Still
and all, he was enough convinced of the value of the
opera to sing the tenor part both in the partial performance of *Villon* in 1924 and in the first complete
performance in 1926.

The instrumentation was altered in accordance
with suggestions by George Antheil; a clavichord,
wind instruments, a violin, and an original medieval
horn (that had only two notes, one very low and another only a bit higher) were added. Tinayre's brother
Paul played the horn for the performance. The British
Broadcasting Corporation (B.B.C.) broadcast the opera
in 1931 and again in 1962.

Pound developed his own theory of opera and
was convinced that in order to achieve a masterly
combination of words and music he must seriously
begin to compose himself. This turned out to be a
self-delusion, an example of how he was increasingly
prone to misjudgments and false conclusions.

There is no doubt that Pound had at his disposal
an excellent ear for the natural cadence of speech and
for the potentials in musical effectives of the spoken
word; in addition, he had acquired an impressive
knowledge of music history and had developed an im-
pelling need to hear good music. (It is for this reason
that he later, while living in Rapallo, initiated and
organized a concert series that drew the foremost mu-

sical performers of the world to the little Italian re-
sort.)

All of this together, however, did not make him
a composer. Pound was infallible in judging the strong
and weak points of others' talents, but he was often
unable to assess his own abilities.

His composing, his work for the myriad little
magazines (Pound had in the meantime become correspondent for *The Dial*); the strain of Parisian life
in the sidewalk cafes of St. Germain des Près, in the
book shop of Sylvia Beach, at the parties of Peggy
Guggenheim; the correspondence in behalf of the
"right" economic policies, which had by now reached
truly grotesque proportions (Pound wrote letters to
ministers, secretaries of finance, and other government
officials of practically every European country, to the
Pope, presidents, kings and judges)—all of this activity
did not diminish Pound's poetic output. A book of
poems that he had written between 1918 and 1921 appeared in the latter year. His letters during this period
are full of thoughts and ideas for the *Cantos*.

Pound himself did not clarify his thoughts about
the *Cantos* for a long time. Three, which were printed
as early as 1917, he regarded as a false start; later, he
withdrew and rewrote them. The final plan, if it can
be said there is one, grew organically during the writing itself. Whether or not such organic growth is a
feasible method for so large and comprehensive an
undertaking, he admittedly did not know.

Cantos that he released for print he always desig-
nated as "drafts." The eighth canto had been printed
by May, 1922 (in *The Dial*) and the twelfth by July
of the following year (in *Criterion*). "The first eleven
cantos are preparation of the palette," Pound wrote
to Professor Shelling.[2] Other letters make it clear that
he hoped to write some hundred to two hundred can-

tos before regarding the work as complete; he reck-
oned that this would take him about forty years.

Pound continued his prose writing as well. Collections of essays were published: *Pavannes and Divisions* in 1918 and *Instigations* in 1920. In 1923, *Indiscretions* appeared, an imaginative autobiography that
covers up to his sixteenth year of age. Pound worked
continually, restlessly, and often desultorily. Life in
Paris was not satisfying to him; he found ever more
facets of it to criticize. He took trips to Italy, at first
for reasons of health; the necessity of undergoing sur-
gery was an added source of discomfort.

In his letters of this period, Pound expresses a
growing discontent with the same poverty of cultural
life in Paris that he had experienced in London. The
air of culture that those who liked to be considered
"literary" gave themselves was repugnant to him. He
believed that all one could do was to continue to
travel eastward if one was to remain mentally and
culturally alive. For the time being, he contented himself with a more intensive study of Confucian thought.
The *XIII Canto,* which Pound wrote in 1923, is dedicated to that great philosopher; from this time, in
fact, his dicta and ideas are very often to be found in
the *Cantos.*

Pound's letters are, aside from being a source of
biographical information, both amusing and informa-
tive from the point of view of style and language. By
the use of phonetic spelling Pound successfully apes
the accent and regional colloquialisms of a wide variety of America's social strata: the country hick, the
provincial small-towner, the one-track-minded busi-
nessman, the farmer, the Negro, the Jew from the
garment district of New York, the lady of good Boston stock. All of these speak in his letters.

Pound had an ear for and a love of dialect.

"Greeks," he remarked in one letter, "I believe, had the decency to spell as it sounded to 'em, even if on two sides of the same street. Bloke said to me yesterday: nine separate dialects in Genoa."[3]

As one reads through the collected letters, however, it is difficult to escape the conclusion that this aping develops into a mannerism. It occurs excessively and often when uncalled for or even out of place. One who is well acquainted with Pound's letters, therefore, takes a more critical view of the poet's use of dialects in the *Cantos* and draws the conclusion that Pound's expressed aim, the preciseness of the word, is thwarted thereby, sometimes even perverted into an unreflected lack of preciseness. Colloquialisms are not often representative of the clearest or most logical thought.

The case for the use of foreign words and phrases in the *Cantos* is even more problematic when seen from the vantage point of their use in the letters. They are there in abundance—French, Italian, Latin, Greek, now and then German—and one is tempted to think it is again Pound's love of exact definition that prompts him to their use.

Kenner says, "The whole key to Pound, the basis of his *Cantos*, his music, his economics, and everything else, is this concern for exact definition."[4] "Le mot juste." And there definitely are words that cannot be translated adequately, let alone exactly.

In the letters, Pound often makes a point with a foreign expression that he could scarcely have hit at all with what passes for the English equivalent. These triumphs of Pound's linguistic versatility can, of course, be appreciated only by the linguistically versatile, but they are quite objectively present.

On the other hand, he uses a foreign phrase just as often when the English equivalent would have been not only adequate but exact, sometimes when the English equivalent would have, for this reader, been a better choice. In these cases, he is both incomprehensible to his reader and untrue to his principles regarding exactness of definition.

Perhaps it was more, or at least just as important to him to give ample evidence of his linguistic versatility.

What can be the advantage of "serieusement" over "seriously"?[5] Wherein is "I must have qualche cosa di speciale" more precise than "some very special things"?[6] Is an Italian exclamation necessarily more expressive than an English one at the end of "That is the crime and the 'obscenity.' E poi basta"?[7] Why the concluding learned air for a sentence so simple as "I will explain sometime viva voce"?[8] What is the difference at all between the English and the French for "15 years plus agée que moi"?[9]

One could go on with example after example of such usages. Their very number prompts the question whether it is not in direct contradiction to the interests of good language to affect such a mélange without sound cause. Is it not rather a sign of mental laziness, for the purposes of letter writing perhaps excusable, a putting down of the word that *first comes to mind* without even looking for a better one or the right one in another language? Pound lived abroad and moved in international circles; the first word to come to his mind would quite naturally not always have been an English one.

The examples given here have been in the Romance languages, which Pound studied, from which he translated, and which, it is strongly to be assumed, he had mastered. (This reader is not versed enough in those languages to say. Some philologists, as has been noted, doubted it.) Pound had definitely not mastered German. Unfortunately, he neither avoids using it nor

bothers to check for errors to make up for his insuf-
ficiency. There are minor ones that he might easily
have checked like the ending in " 'Das Neues Leben'
and other operas."[10] "Das neue Leben" is correct.

More serious, however, are instances in which
Pound attempts to make a didactic point or a linguistic distinction, that is, to teach his reader something by
means of a German word or expression whose definition he does not know and which he misuses. Pound
writes, for example, in a letter to Ronald Duncan:

Admitting *all* the to put it mildly *im*perfections of the race of
nuvvelists, of teas; but to edit, to speak *to,* to *aus*gaben, as dis-
tinct from meditatin' on the old umbilicus??? *If* that mechanism
isn't used by the young they got to invent some other. If no
donkey cart, a wheelbarrow. . . .[11]

The word "Ausgaben" is the plural of "Ausgabe,"
which means "edition," an edition of a book. Pound
has given this noun the plural ending, which looks
like, but isn't, a verb ending. Taking it for a verb, he
doesn't capitalize it. As a verb, the word doesn't exist
at all. What Pound wants is "herausgeben," that is, as
he says correctly in English, "to edit." Of course, what
Pound is after here is the plasticity of the German
prefix "aus" as opposed to "in," the editors being ex-
troverted, rather than introverted, like the novelists.
But he could have had it with the "heraus" as well,
had he known the correct expression. Witticisms in
the vicinity of this kind of blunder somehow don't
seem so witty.

Such instances are unfortunately not confined to
the letters. Were it so, they would not find mention
here. In his prose book *ABC of Reading,* Pound is
seriously advising the literarily interested and talented
in methods of self-education that teach the essential
and are potentially fruitful. He opposes these methods to those current in institutional education that he

considers perverted and barren. He writes, "A people that grows accustomed to sloppy writing is a people in process of losing grip on its empire and itself."[12]

He goes on to justify the use of many languages in art: "The sum of human wisdom is not contained in any one language, and no single language is CAPABLE of expressing all forms and degrees of human comprehension."[13]

Two pages later, he sets up a rather racist defense, "You receive the language as your race has left it, the words have meanings which have 'grown into the race's skin'; the Germans say 'wie in den Schnabel gewachsen,' as it grows in his beak."

The German saying is both misquoted and misinterpreted. Pound has probably only heard it and not read it; he gives us "in" for "ihm" and "den" for "der." Had he looked it up, he could have at least quoted it correctly. It is used to describe a most unaffected and natural manner of speech.

A person who talks "wie ihm der Schnabel gewachsen ist" does exactly what Pound does not do. He puts on no airs, affects no learnedness, no pose, uses no circumlocutions, no embellishments. He speaks a straightforward, simple language every man must understand. He speaks "the way his beak naturally grows." This saying can in no way refer to any racial or even national characteristic. Isn't this sloppy thinking?

If such errors hurt a book with didactic intentions, what can be said when they creep into Pound's poetry, into what is, in the final analysis, the most important of his work? *Canto LI* is, for this reader, a masterly poem, with lines like:

> With usury the stone cutter is kept
>     from his stone
> the weaver is kept from his loom by
>     usura

> Wool does not come into market
> the peasant does not eat his own grain
> the girl's needle goes blunt in her hand
> The looms are hushed one after another
> ten thousand after ten thousand.

Why does Pound encumber it with:

> Thus speaking in Königsberg
> Zwischen die Völkern erzielt wird
> a modus vivendi.

where again the German is wrong? Who knows what he means? Either it's "zwischen die Völker" cr "zwischen den Völkern," but under no circumstances is it what Pound has used.

Let us be thankful we have not the knowledge to check Pound's Chinese. In ignorance of the errors, we can at least appreciate the surrounding beauties. It is not without some skepticism, however, that we can regard the polyglot characteristics of the *Cantos*. Can they be defended for artistic reasons?

The foreign-language elements in the *Cantos* are for the most part quotations. Pound quotes from the most diverse sources: the troubadours, Dante, Greek mythology, Homer, Plotin, Catullus, Chaucer, Elizabethan poets and dramatists, to name only some. A complete list of these sources would, according to Pound's design for the *Cantos,* be an approximate pinpointing of the highest cultural achievements of mankind. He retains the original language and form of the quotations in order to mirror, or to summon up, the unadulterated spirit of the epoch of their origin.

If these quotations did not appear in the original, it would be necessary to write volumes in order to approximate or describe the spirit that they embody as only great literature can. And this is Pound's design. He wants to parade before his reader the whole pageant of the history of mankind while calling to life the constant elements in that great flow, the highest cultural achievements of the epochs and the nations, those that are timeless and immortal. He wants to preserve in his songs what he calls the permanent basis in humanity.

Pound treats these highpoints as simultaneous moments that happen to differ from one another by mechanical chronology but not in inner value. Their external, superficial characteristics, their form, their language, differ, but not the degree of their beauty. With this method of seeing man's highest achievements as "simultaneous" in the sense of their timelessness, Pound comes close to the systematic thought of contemporary philosophers of history, like Spengler and Toynbee, who at that time were developing their theories.

Pound has often been asked whether or not he considered the polyglot elements of the *Cantos* a hindrance to their comprehensibility. He has given different answers to different people at different times. An oft-repeated answer is that the quotations are explained within the *Cantos* themselves.

Skip anything you don't understand and go on till you pick it up again. All tosh about *foreign languages* making it difficult. The quotes are all either explained at once by repeat or they are definitely *of* the things indicated. If reader don't know what an elefant IS, then the word is obscure.

I admit there are a couple of Greek quotes, one along in [Canto] 39 that can't be understood without Greek, but *if* I can drive the reader to learning at least that much Greek, she or he will indubitably be filled with a durable gratitude. And if not, what harm? I can't conceal the fact that the Greek language existed.[14]

Another answer, however, was that it isn't absolutely necessary to understand these quotations to understand the sense of the whole. The sense of the whole exists independently of the quotations. Then again he has said that most of the quotations are either translated or interpreted immediately upon their appearance in the canto in question. For instance, the Chinese ideograms are followed by a transliteration of their pronunciation and an English equivalent of their meaning.

Pound's overall design of historical synthesis is readily apprehensible. Images, names, figures of diverse cultural origin appear in sequence, old gods in juxtaposition to new ones. Pound manifests his belief in the mythical fundament of all civilizations. Like Frobenius, Frazer, or Jung, he sees the comparability of all mythical figures. Whether, however, Pound's verses are apprehensible to a reader who is not overly familiar with Robert Browning, with the poetry of certain Chinese or Japanese poets, with the paintings of Picasso, with the wording of Homer or Ovid, remains an open question. These verses afford at any rate *active* participation on the part of the reader. Most commentaries on the *Cantos* begin with a body of explanation, and there is a whole book of reference that was compiled in an attempt to explain every allusion in Ezra Pound's *Cantos*.[15]

To read the *Cantos* with this key, however, is to gain the parts while losing the whole. One solves the crossword puzzle instead of appreciating the poem. Hugh Kenner gives the better method for reading the *Cantos,* that is, to read them with a calm and open mind, to allow the associations to come into being; they are "apprehensible, not explicable."[16]

The first book of cantos appeared in Paris in 1925 *(A Draft of XVI Cantos).* In the same year, Pound left the French capital and moved to Rapallo. He had often spent time there for reasons of health, but his decision to finally take up residence in Italy was prompted by a genuine affection for the people and the landscape. He continues his work on the *Cantos;* the second volume, *A Draft of Cantos 17-27,* was printed in London in 1928, and the third, *A Draft of XXX Cantos,* two years later in Paris.

Finally, in Rapallo, Pound founded his own little magazine, *The Exile;* he now had the opportunity of printing whatever he wrote without the preliminaries of acceptance by a publishing organ, and also without the critical censure that such procedures entail.

In this magazine, T. S. Eliot's *Criterion,* in *The New Review, The English Journal, Poetry, The New English Weekly, The Egoist, Little Review, New Age,* and others still, Pound carried on his crusade for the undelayed adoption and execution of the politico-economic system of Douglas and Gesell. He propagated these ideas, too, in purely scientific or technical journals like the Italian *Rassegna Monetaria,* in communistically oriented journals like *New Masses,* in journals that were under Fascist influence, like the Australian *New Times,* and in magazines for the Japanese, for American Negroes, and for the Armed Forces.

It must have been a matter of indifference to Pound with which sects, parties, racial prejudices, or group biases he identified himself by using these organs as his mouthpiece, for he published indiscriminately in journals whose orientations were in direct opposition one to the other. For this reason, it is false to attempt to prove any sympathy on Pound's part for the policies they represented by the fact that he published in any one.

Not enough that Pound bombarded magazines with his articles on economics; he wrote, in addition, literally thousands of letters to persons of influence to set his ideas through. He was of a burning impatience in such matters. He persistently thought he was on the brink of finding someone who would listen and could act. As time went on, this became—it can be called nothing else—an obsession.

During the decade of the 1930s, Pound wrote in this behalf to Mrs. Roosevelt, to members of the Roosevelt cabinet, to chairmen of Senate committees, to eminent bankers like James Paul Warburg, to authors, poets, learned men, et cetera. He received answers above all from biased interest groups that supplied him with their propaganda brochures.

Since he had been living abroad, and especially since he had taken up residence in Rapallo, Pound had succeedingly lost contact with his former friends and acquaintances in the U.S., England and France; he therefore became increasingly susceptible to the—at best—distorted and often outrightly deceptive accounts in these journals. He writes about and quotes from them as though they printed serious documents of fact.

Pound did make one attempt to gather information independently and directly. He mailed out a questionnaire that was headed "Volitionist Economics." It contained questions as to taxes, currencies, labor, paper money, and property that were worded so as to give the compiler an overall view of the opinions on these issues of those questioned.

Engagement in money matters, it must be remembered, was a family tradition with the Pounds. Ezra's paternal grandfather had already supported a bill for money reform in Congress in the nineteenth century. And Ezra's father, in his turn, had been assayer at the mint.

In the first of a series of essays on finance and money themes that Pound wrote in Rapallo between 1935 and 1944 and that were later (1950 ff.) published in England under the title *Money Pamphlets,* Pound relates incidents that he had witnessed while still a child of the good citizens who had been cheated bringing the gold bars they had purchased to his father to be weighed.

Economic and finance reform became a fixed idea with Pound. He allowed himself to become involved in time-consuming and utterly fruitless inner squabbles among the various little money-reform groups. Of sadder consequence was that he now engaged in writing prose the subject matter of which lay wholly outside any literary area. *ABC of Economics* (1933), *Jefferson and/or Mussolini,* and *Social Credit, an Impact* (both 1935) are examples.

Pound's method of historical research, if one can speak of a method here at all, was in every respect insufficient. He extracted, for instance, from the works of Thomas Jefferson whatever fit into his concept, leaving out what didn't fit, and augmenting what he had chosen according to his own preconceived opinion with "facts" and opinions chosen at random from the interest-group publications that were always at his disposal to make a grand total of Poundian proof. Never did he submit the "material" he was using to a close examination. He wrote economics as he wrote poetry, associatively, eclectically.

Whether Pound is speaking of history or of economics, usury is the starting point, central point, and endpoint of the discussion. He seizes upon Rothschild as the prototype of the usurer. His source for this assumption was to a good measure a provocative white-supremacy journal called *Liberation,* published in Asheville, North Carolina.

Pound gives this journal as his source in an article he wrote for the *Little Magazine* entitled "To the Young, If Any." He declares his solidarity with *Liberation*'s point of view that Rothschild was responsible for the Civil War. His subscription to this view appears in almost the same form again in *Canto XLVIII*.

In general, it can be said that Pound's prose of this period parallels or is a commentary to the cantos he was writing. An alleged quotation from Benjamin Franklin that he uses in *Canto LII* is also taken from *Liberation:*

> Remarked Ben: better keep out the jews
> or yr/grand children will curse you
> jews, real jews, chazims, and *reschek*
> *also super-reschek* or the international
> racket

Carl Van Doren calls the speech against the Jews printed in *Liberation* and ascribed to Franklin a forgery.[17]

It is, however, wholly in such spurious matter that Pound's anti-Semitic statements consist. Were it not for the horrors of the Hitler era, they probably would never have received much attention. Of course, Pound lent them a potent accentuation when he identified himself with the Fascism of Mussolini (who was not explicitly anti-Semitic, but allowed Hitler's atrocities within his land). To look for longer, well-founded, or even logical anti-Setimic passages in Pound's work is to be disappointed. Here there are five verses about Rothschild, there a paragraph on the Jews in international finance, often there is invective that Pound has simply copied out of another source. Lore Lenberg points out that Pound just as sporadically has words of praise for Jewish culture and compares Christian culture unfavorably to it.[18]

Pound's anti-Semitism is characteristic of the nationalistic and conservative political tendencies that were to be found in Europe between 1880 and 1914 and that were the compost on which Hitler's active and aggressive anti-Semitism grew.

Pound's liaison with Italian Fascism is another

matter. He saw in Mussolini's political program the only possible hope for the Italian people. He met "il duce" himself only once and futilely tried on that occasion to convince him of his own economic theories.

Pound defends Mussolini's system repeatedly, saying that some people attack it without the least knowledge of conditions or developments in Fascist Italy. Sometimes, his words of praise are written with the deliberate intention of shocking his reader.

Pound dates his letters of this period, for instance, in the Fascist manner, "anno XI dell' era Fascista." At other times, his comments give evidence of genuine esteem. Despite all of this it is wrong to call so pronounced an individualist as Ezra Pound a 100 per cent Fascist. He rejected such a system for the United States.

The type of government that he thought best for the States according to an article that he wrote in 1936, "Our Own Form Of Government," is no more than a continuation of the old democratic tradition, but one that "works." Pound's stumbling block was his oversimplification of theories he was too enthused about to bother thinking through.

The problematic nature of Pound's character is not only to be seen in his attitudes and actions regarding the Jews and the Fascists. His relationship to his son is even more perplexing.

Omar Shakespear Pound was born in the American Hospital in Paris in 1926. The boy was brought to his maternal grandmother in London to live. Dorothy Pound spent a good deal of time in England, visiting with her son and her mother, while her husband was elsewhere. In 1938, when the grandmother died and the Pounds arrived in London to regulate ensuing family matters, Pound met his son. The next time

Omar saw his father was when Pound was arrested for treason and imprisoned in Pisa. Omar was a U.S. soldier stationed in Germany at the time, and it was only by chance that he heard from a comrade the story of the "old man in a cage" in Pisa. He applied for leave and went to Italy.

Pound's relationship to his son is significant; he simply excluded him from his life. His son did not exist for him. Only that which was helpful to Pound, or at least not bothersome, existed in his private life; everything else was negated. This was in direct contradiction to his practice as an artist. No exertion was too great to go through for a young artist whose work Pound recognized as good. And politically he was even more vehemently engaged for his cause than artistically, although with incomparably less well-founded knowledge.

In his family life, he was not capable of a natural measure of affection, not to speak of love; he sought as compensation only that much more recognition from the public.

In the light of the biographical data sketched above, which makes apparent Pound's liability to err in scholarly, political, and personal matters, it wouldn't be difficult to pass devastating judgment on Pound. Lack of judgment, immaturity, and egocentrism would be the accusations that a critic might level on him. But when one adds to the man Pound, the artist, the poet, the literary worker, when one considers Pound's unconditional dedication to the arts, then the picture becomes much more complex than a critic who wishes only to condemn can admit.

It is in keeping with this paradoxical picture that Pound has received both the highest praise and the fewest awards for his work. As schismatic as Pound's personality in itself is, so schismatic is the judgment of

the critics as to the work and the man. There is the
school that affirms him and the school that rejects him;
they hold each other in balance.

In 1922, T. S. Eliot won the prize that *The Dial*
awards for high achievement in American literary arts;
Marianne Moore received it in 1924; E. E. Cummings
in 1925; William Carlos Williams in 1926. Pound had
immeasurably influenced the work of all of these
authors. He himself received the prize after they did,
in 1927. The editors of the magazine even expressed
the fear that he wouldn't accept the award, its belated-
ness being such an affront. He did accept it, but on
the condition that it be specified as a prize for the
*Cantos* or for his poetic works, not for his prose. He
invested the prize money of two thousand dollars in
such a manner as to receive a hundred dollars a year
in interest. Later, he used this money to pay authors
royalties for contributions to his own magazine *The
Exile*.

# 6

*Radio
Rome*

On March 31, 1940, in a letter to Ronald Duncan, Pound writes:

Blasted friends left a goddam radio here yester. Gift. God damn destructive and dispersive devil of an invention. But got to be faced. Drammer has got to face it, not only face cinema. Anybody who *can* survive *may* strengthen inner life, but mass of apes and worms will be still further rejuiced to passivity. Hell a state of passivity? Or limbo?

Anyhow what drammer or teeyater *wuz,* radio is. Possibly the loathing of it may stop diffuse writing. No sense in print *until* it gets to finality? Also the histrionic developments in announcing. And the million to one chance that audition will develop: at least to a faculty for picking the fake in the voices. Only stuff fit to hear was Tripoli, Sofia and Tunis. Howling music in two of 'em and a cembalo in Bugarea.

And a double sense of the blessedness of silence when the damn thing is turned off.

Anyhow, if you're writin for styge or teeyater up to date, you gotter measure it all, not merely against cinema, but much more against the personae now poked into every bleedin' 'ome and smearing the mind of the peepull. If anyone is a purrfekk HERRRRkules, he may survive, and *may* clarify his style in *resistance* to the devil box. I mean if he ain't druv to melancolia crepitans before he recovers.

I anticipated the damn thing in first third of Cantos and was able to do 52/71 because I was the last survivin' monolith who did not have a bloody radio in the 'ome. However, like the subjects of sacred painting as Mr. Cohen said: "Vot I say iss, we got to svallow 'em, vot I say iss, ve got to svallow 'em." Or be boa-constricted.[1]

Pound saw in the "devil's box" with which he became acquainted at so late a date both a challenge and a destructive influence for the artist. Radio was to prove destructive for Pound. At the beginning, however, it was a challenge, mainly to his drive for recognition and esteem, in particular for the recognition and esteem of America.

Thirty years of exile had strengthened in Pound

the desire to be called home a famous and celebrated man. In 1939, Pound was fifty-four years old. He had up to then not been honored by America in a form that could possibly have satisfied either his vanity or his pride.

In the face of Pound's real significance for English and most specifically American poetry, the little prize from *The Dial* as the sole token of distinction in all those long years seems a bitter irony. Pound's deeply felt disappointment was justified. A prize would have helped financially too.

Pound had always struggled to live on his royalties. He had received no fee for the greater part of his work as literary adviser to, and correspondent for so many magazines. Pound had seen to it that other writers received the means to continue their work. No one had done the same for him. What money he did earn he had to bargain for or beg of his publishers and editors, a fact that is abundantly documented by numerous letters of supplication.

But financial means for personal needs were really secondary for Pound; he lived on literary recognition—which, from the nation of his birth, was wanting.

Without summons, without invitation, full of determination "to wake America up," Pound set out for home in April 1939. A little inheritance that had come from Dorothy's mother financed the trip. His choice of travel accommodations reveals a great deal about his feelings at this time; he sailed first class in a luxury suite. This is the way he wanted to arrive in New York. He was interviewed by a reporter on board the Italian ship *Rex* even before docking.

Pound was granted an honorary doctor's degree in June from Hamilton College, his alma mater. Another ex-Hamiltonian, Professor H. W. Thompson of Cornell University, had written an article in praise of

Pound, and it is likely that the idea of honoring him in this way arose through this article. What happened at the banquet given at Hamilton on the occasion is characteristic of the events of this whole trip.

H. V. Kaltenborn, the well-known news commentator, was the invited speaker of the evening. He carried forth at length on democracy and democratic countries and made reference to the "doubtful alliance" between Italy and Germany. Pound interrupted him to ask what he meant by "doubtful." The speaker began to explain, but Pound interrupted once more and lost himself in rapturous praise of Mussolini in particular and Fascism in general. Kaltenborn responded with the trite observation that, thank God, one could still freely voice even such opinions in the United States of America. This reply was, of course, in no way satisfactory to Pound.

As his retorts grew more aggressive, he was finally told that it was, at best, unseemly conduct to utter such antidemocratic opinions in the halls of an American college. This comment received applause from the assembled guests who were there to honor Pound. The quarrel threatened to explode, but the dean of the college put an end to it.

In his own speech, which then followed, Pound declared that his books and articles about the economic malady of the United States must be considered compulsory, prerequisite reading for everybody.

During the six months that Pound spent in the U.S., such scenes occurred repeatedly. Sometimes they were of less, sometimes of more import; some were private affairs, others public. He spoke with Henry A. Wallace, who was later to become Vice President under Roosevelt. He sought out professors, clergymen, bankers, senators, and congressmen and tried to make it clear to each of them that the present fallacious economic policy of the United States had brought the country to the brink of catastrophe. It was not the impending war he was referring to; on the contrary, he expressly predicted that there would be no World War II, as it must be apparent to all that this would be sheer madness. He visited his old friends and acquaintances and snowed them under with lectures about Fascism, Silvio Gesell, and "goddamned Jewry."

Norman says, "Pound brought his enthusiasm for fascism, his theories on economics and his anti-Semitism. He was not a welcome visitor; friends of a lifetime shut their doors on him in disgust; the most charitable view was that he was a sick man."[2]

Pound returned to Rapallo in the late summer of 1939. In February 1940, he made his first broadcast in English for Radio Rome. He had himself asked for permission to make the broadcast and spoke over the "American Hour," which was received in the U.S. as well as in Europe. This was the first of some seventy-five broadcasts that Pound wrote for the broadcasting station. They asked that he continue them after the first one and assured him that he would enjoy complete freedom of opinion. The broadcasts were preceeded by the announcement,

Radio Rome, . . . following the tradition of Italian hospitality, . . . has offered Dr. Ezra Pound the use of the microphone twice a week. It is understood that he will not be asked to say anything whatsoever that goes against his conscience, or anything incompatible with his duties as a citizen of the U.S.A.[3]

When Pound wanted to visit the U.S. again in the summer of 1941, he was denied entry by the American consulate in Rome because he was an advocate of Fascism. Pound's comment on this in a broadcast was, "As a writer I am given to no one and to all men." As late as December 7, 1941, but before the declaration of war, Pound spoke warningly in his broadcast about the insanity of war. On December 8, after Pearl Harbor and the American declaration of war on Japan, Radio Rome terminated Pound's broadcasts for reasons of security. They thought it not impossible that Pound would transmit codified secret information for his native country by means of his ad-libbing and verbose broadcasting style that was a hopeless mixture of phrases in dialect, quotations and citations, words and expressions in any number of foreign tongues; in a word: uncheckable.

Having thus come under suspicion of espionage against the system he supported, Pound was inclined to leave Italy for the duration of the war. (In the meantime, Italy and Germany had declared war on the U.S.)

He and his wife made preparations to return "home" and wanted to leave Italy on a special train that had been provided to take American diplomats and journalists and their families out of enemy territory. But American officials in Rome refused to grant him permission to board and told him the U.S. government had declared him *persona non grata*. That was in February 1942.

In April of that year, *Poetry* magazine, which owed its literary reputation and quality to Ezra Pound, published an editorial entitled "The End of Ezra Pound." The magazine disrupted irrevocably all connections with Pound because, "the broadcasts, which he continues to make, have become deliberate attempts to undermine the country of his birth through enemy propaganda."

Pound began to broadcast for Radio Rome again about this time; more exactly, he was again permitted by the Italian government and in turn the broadcasting company to do so. These broadcasts had been monitored in Great Britain and the U.S. from their incipience. The texts were scrutinized for treasonable passages by the Foreign Broadcast Intelligence Service. In July 1943, the District Court of the U.S. issued a true bill of indictment against Pound. The charge of treason was upheld by a jury.

Pound protested against this condemnation *in absentia*. He wrote a long letter in his own defense to Francis Biddle, then U.S. Attorney General. Pound said,

I have not spoken with regard to *this* war, but in protest against a system which creates one war after another, in series and in system.

He maintained: "The whole basis of democracy or majority government assures that the citizen shall be informed of the facts." He considered it his duty to inform the American people: "a man's duties increase with his knowledge." He argued: "Free speech under modern conditions becomes a mockery if it does not include the right to free speech over the radio." In addition, he stated: "The assumption of the right to punish and take vengeance regardless of the area of jurisdiction is dangerous. I do not mean in a small way; but for the nation."[4]

If Pound had given up his American citizenship and become an Italian citizen, he could probably have avoided the indictment for treason; he was informed of this. He rejected such a step categorically and energetically, saying that his actions were in accord with and in support of the American Constitution and the true principles of democracy.

Just what did Pound say in these broadcasts? What was the information that he considered it his democratic duty to transmit to the American people at so great a risk? On February 3, 1942:

You are at war for the duration of the Germans' pleasure. You are at war for the duration of Japan's pleasure. Nothing in the

Western world, nothing in the whole of our occident can help
you dodge that. Nothing can help you dodge it.

### On April 16, 1942:

For the United States to be making war on Italy and on Europe
is just plain damn nonsense, and every native-born American
of American stock knows that it is plain downright damn nonsense. And for this state of things Franklin Roosevelt is more
than any other one man responsible.

### On April 23, 1942:

Of course for you to go looking for my point—points of my bi-
weekly talk in a maze of Jew-governed American radio transmis-
sions—is like looking for one needle in a whole flock of hay-
stacks.

### On May 5, 1942:

Europe callin'—Pound speakin' . . . The kike, and the un-
mitigated evil that has been centered in London since the
British government set on the Red Indians to murder the American frontier settlers, has herded the Slavs, the Mongols, the
Tartar openly against Germany and Poland and Finland. And
secretly against all that is decent in America, against the total
American heritage.

### On July 22, 1942:

And how much liberty have you got, anyhow? And as to the
arsenal—are you the arsenal of democracy or of judeocracy? And
who rules your rulers? Where does public responsibility end and
what races can mix in America without ruin of the American
stock, the American brain?

### On May 4, 1943:

What are you doing in the war at all? What are you doing in
Africa? . . . Every day of war is a dead day as well as a death
day. More death, more future servitude, less and less of American
liberty of any variety.

In between such comments, Pound told his listeners anecdotes, held forth on the wisdom of Confucius, and gave proof of the misguided state of

American economics. He attacked his friend Archibald MacLeish, who was Undersecretary of State at the time, saying:

I asked Archie to say openly why he handed out four billion dollars in excess profits on the gold . . . between 1932 and 1940, handing it to a dirty gang of kikes and hyper-kikes on the London gold exchange firms.

He said, if America's youth had "had the sense to eliminate Roosevelt and his Jews or the Jews and their Roosevelt at the last election, you would not now be at war." Often, he voiced the suspicion that his broadcasts could not be heard in America at all because the networks were dominated by Jews.

In general, Pound stayed on any one theme only for a few sentences and then left it to go on to another. His broadcasts were marked by prolix abuse and outbursts of anger; nothing was thought through, everything was without design and disorganized. As he said himself on March 8, 1942, "I lose my thread at times, so much that I can't count on anyone's mind."

Pound's motives? To look for a rational motivation would be to look in vain. The broadcasts are the culminating point of an evolutionary process. For more than a decade, Pound had been propagating his economic and political theories, indiscriminately and with impunity, through any organ that offered itself without the least regard for the potential consequences of having associated himself with the one or the other. For over three decades, Pound had been in the habit of seeing his ideas effect sensation and shock. His new thoughts about poetry had at the time caused no less astonishment than his political ideas. For more than four decades, Pound had lived outside the pale of normally accepted bourgeois mores. He had always gone his own way, and his ways had always been strange ones.

But he had always possessed a strong faith in his ends, and this was true now, too. Pound believed, with an almost religious fervor, that usury ruled the world, that America would be able to reapproach the original spirit of her own Constitution if she would only take Italy as her guide. Of course, a personality like Pound's was always precariously close to the border of charlatanry; his vanity and his need for recognition were always vying for the upper hand with his good common sense; in the end, it was unfortunately not his good common sense that won out.

How little the Axis countries, for their part, valued Pound's "cooperation" became clear in the spring of 1944 when the Pounds were turned out of their house in Rapallo to make way for the German troops who were fortifying the beach with bunkers. Pound retired to an old house in Sant Ambrogio. On the first floor, an olive press was running all day. On the second, Pound was translating the works of Meng-tsu, a disciple of Confucius. He was arrested there by the American troops who took Italy in 1945.

Pound was interned in the Disciplinary Training Center of the American Forces in Pisa. This was a camp surrounded by barbed wire where GI deserters, rapists, murderers, assault-and-battery convicts, and other criminals were detained. Some of them were hanged in Aversa. Others were deported to penitentiaries and jails in the U.S. Some could rehabilitate themselves through work and good behavior.

Pound was the one and only civilian internee. He was imprisoned in one of the open steel-wire cages that were provided for particularly hard to handle disciplinary cases. His was the last such cage in a row. They were open so that such "trainees," as the prisoners were called, could be under observation at all times.

Pound was completely isolated. None of his

friends and no member of his family was notified of his whereabouts. None of the soldiers or other prisoners was allowed to talk to him. During the day, he fell victim to the sun and the dust, at night to the cold. After a few days, he was granted a small tent in which to sleep. He set it up inside his cage in what the other trainees called an ingenious manner. The cage was brightly lighted all night long. Wrapped in blankets, Pound slept on the concrete floor. During the day, he paced his square of the great world. Two guards were assigned to him at all times. A Negro, who brought him his food, sometimes spoke to him—in violation of regulations. He was permitted to keep his copy of Confucius, and a pen and paper, but no typewriter. The physical exercises that he took daily made him the sensation of the camp. Everyone came to watch him shadow box, fence, and play tennis. Then someone gave him a broomstick, which he used alternately as a baseball bat, tennis racket, floret, and billiard cue.

That way he fooled the camp psychiatrist on being examined increased his reputation as an eccentric. For hours on end, he contemplated the doings of the ants, the wasps building their nest, the oxen plodding the old Viareggio road.

After three weeks, Pound collapsed from amnesia, claustrophobia, and hysteria. His eyes were inflamed from the sun and the dust. He was taken from the cage and put in a tent in the sick section, which was, comparably, a little more comfortable. The Negro built him—in violation of regulations—a table. The doctors lent him a typewriter and even talked to him.

In October, when he had been in prison for six months, Ezra Pound celebrated his sixtieth birthday, an occasion on which poets and writers whose works are doomed to oblivion are usually honored and celebrated. No one took note of the birthday of Ezra Pound.

In October, too, Pound was allowed to receive a visit from his family. On November 8, he was transported to Washington by air.

Army officers who have been questioned as to the reasons for Pound's having been imprisoned in this degrading manner offer as an explanation that it was greatly feared that Pound's allies would attempt to free him forcibly. Since Pound was taken prisoner after the unconditional surrender of these "allies," Italy and Germany, the explanation strikes one as insincere to say the least.

Pound wrote of his inner experiences during the months in Pisa in his *Pisan Cantos*. The rise and fall of his spirits is painfully manifest in these poems: the humanity of the animals, the animality of the humans, life and speech in the camp, monologues, soliloquies, new thoughts about old thoughts, moments of insight into self:

> The ant's a centaur in his dragon world.
> Pull down thy vanity, it is not man
> Made courage, or made order, or made grace,
>     Pull down thy vanity, I say pull down.
> Learn of the green world what can be thy place
> In scaled invention or true artistry,
> Pull down thy vanity,
>                     Paquin pull down!
> The green casque has outdone your elegance.
>
> "Master thyself, then others shall thee beare"
>     Pull down thy vanity
> Thou art a beaten dog beneath the hail,
> A swollen magpie in a fitful sun,
> Half black half white
> Nor knowst'ou wing from tail
> Pull down thy vanity
>                     How mean thy hates

Fostered in falsity,
            Pull down thy vanity,
Rathe to destroy, niggard in charity,
Pull down thy vanity,
            I say pull down.

But to have done instead of not doing
            this is not vanity
To have, with decency, knocked
That a Blunt should open
            To have gathered from the air a live tradition
or from a fine old eye the unconquered flame
This is not vanity.
            Here error is all in the not done,
all in the diffidence that faltered,[5]

In Washington, Pound was again indicted for treason. After their initial conversations with Pound, his lawyers came to the conclusion that he was still suffering from the effects of his nervous breakdown in Pisa.

Pound spoke confusedly, jumped from one subject to another; he was not capable of grasping the full import of his situation and maintained that President Truman and other high officials of government, with whom he had had absolutely no contact, would receive him, would help him—if he could only speak to them once to get his economic theories across to them. When one lawyer asked him how he felt about their pleading insanity on his behalf, he said the thought had already occurred to him.

Pound was submitted to psychiatric examination upon order of the court. The doctors found that he was "mentally incompetent to stand trial; of unsound mind." It was on the basis of these findings that Pound was committed to St. Elizabeth's Hospital for therapy. He was to be brought to trial after the successful completion of this psychiatric treatment. The decision of the doctors was read before the court on February 13, 1946.

One year later, Pound's attorneys attempted to convince the court that their mandate's state of mental health had not changed, that it would not change, and that Pound, therefore, would be condemned to confinement in St. Elizabeth's for the rest of his life if charges were not dropped. The plea was denied. Repeated pleas in this vein during the following years were equally unsuccessful. Pound remained an inmate at St. Elizabeth's for twelve years.

His wife visited him daily during this time. First, she lived with her son in the vicinity; later, she took rooms nearer the hospital. One of Pound's biographers, Mullins, who was for three years also a daily visitor, gave the following description:

It is difficult to convey in words the sordid horror of the situation in which Pound spent a considerable portion of his life— the rank, dead odor, the atmosphere of futility as the blank faced old men paced up and down the hall, the sense of utter hopelessness.[6]

Mullins, however, had seen only the second station to which Pound was brought in the hospital, the so-called "chestnut station" for senile males. Before that, he had been in a station that was known as the "hell hole" where the dangerously insane were held. The directors of the hospital never made an unequivocal statement as to what mental illness Pound was actually being treated for; finally, they called him frankly a political prisoner.

Persons who visited Pound during these twelve years describe him as completely normal, even jovial and optimistic.

He seemed cheerful and energetic. This was his way of withstanding the hell into which Fate, as the Federal Government is sometimes known, had deposited him. During the ensuing decade, I seldom saw one of his visitors who was so filled with vitality and optimism as himself.[7]

Pound had many visitors, young writers and painters, representatives of the various sects and political groups with which he had corresponded for so long (for example the "Seaboard White Citizens' Council," which propagated in its brochures the economic theories of Gottfried Feder, Hitler's one-time economic adviser).

Even here, Pound remained true to his principle (or to his old habit) of helping young artists who were in financial straits; he put aside a bit of his food from each meal for them. Pound had himself practically no means of support. His lawyer had collected money from his friends. He could live on his royalties no better than he ever could, although by this time he had published more than thirty books.

In 1948, New Directions published Cantos LXXIV–LXXXIV, *The Pisan Cantos.* In February 1949, Pound was awarded the Bollingen Prize for this work. The prize included a donation of one thousand dollars. That this award, which was granted by the U.S. Library of Congress, was given to a poet who was under indictment for treason against the United States for works that had been written during his imprisonment for that crime loosed a storm of protest that was without precedent in literary history. The jury that had chosen Pound consisted of honorary members, "fellows in American Letters of the Library of Congress; they were such esteemed writers as Conrad Aiken, W. H. Auden, T. S. Eliot, Robert Lowell, Katherine Anne Porter, Karl Shapiro, Allan Tate, Robert Penn Warren, Archibald MacLeish, and William Carlos Williams.

The award went to the poet who in the estimation of this jury had made the greatest achievement in the field of American poetry that year. Under no circum-

stances can these men be suspected of having right-
wing (or "Fascist") political tendencies; on the contrary, most of them held liberal to left-wing views. In
answer to the numerous and vehement attacks by the
American press and certain congressmen, the jury
offered an official statement that ended:

To permit other considerations than that of poetic achievement
to sway the decision would destroy the significance of the award
and would in principle deny the validity of that objective perception of value on which civilized society must rest.[8]

This statement, sad to say, in no way ended the
protests, and although the prize had been awarded for
a work of art, *The Pisan Cantos,* the accusations, as
well as the retorts, took on the character of an evaluation of Ezra Pound the man and the poet. In the last
analysis, the question posed was whether or not it is
possible to separate a writer's expressed political view-
points from his work. If so, was such a distinction
possible in the case of Ezra Pound since his politics
were by his own choice an integral part of his poems?

Even where this was affirmed the further question
arose, whether or not the United States government,
under whose auspices the prize was after all granted,
could afford to identify itself with the anti-Semitic
statements and the arguments in support of Fascism
to be found in the *Pisan Cantos,* especially in the light
of the fact that this government had, for such statements, indicted Ezra Pound for treason.

There are not many nations on this earth in which
such a discussion could even take place. Quite aside
from the question as to whether or not the American
authors who chose Pound for the award acted in the
best political or aesthetic interests, their civil courage
is to be admired. It shrunk back neither before the
government nor before what is known as public
opinion.

The situation will hardly arise again even in the

United States. The Bollingen Award was given by the Library of Congress for the first and last time in 1948. After that, the responsibility for awarding the prize was left to Yale University, a private institution.

The writers and critics who either attacked or defended Pound in this controversy and a number of whom in essays, articles, and open letters petitioned the government to pardon Pound, granted him thereby exactly that sort of recognition and esteem that he had hungered after during his entire career.

The sensation of Pound's martyrdom and the award that followed upon it, ridiculously belated and even then controversial, had a greater effect than any sensation he had produced in his youth, whether the eccentrically bohemian dress of the London era, the literary movements from imagist to *BLAST,* or the public battles from *The Waste Land* to *Ulysses.* Over and above this, the newspaper and magazine articles touching the Bollingen Award were often serious evaluations of Pound's artistic work. Paradoxically, Ezra Pound had to become a traitor to his country in order to reap its honors.

The attempt to have Pound released from St. Elizabeth's finally bore fruit ten years after the Bollingen affair in April 1958. The charges against him were dropped. With his wife, Ezra Pound returned to Italy, to the vicinity of Merano. He was seventy-two years old. Archibald MacLeish, Robert Frost, E. E. Cummings, William Carlos Williams, T. S. Eliot, and Ernest Hemingway had played decisive roles in obtaining his pardon. But many others, too many to name here, had worked in his behalf. Perhaps the one man to whom the most credit for Pound's final release must be given was Archibald MacLeish, the man whom Pound had so unjustifiedly attacked in his Rome broadcasts.

Works that Pound completed in the hospital and

after his release have since appeared. His lifework, *The Cantos,* to which he has added at intervals, is still incomplete.

The discussion as to the final value of his work continues both in the United States and abroad: genius or charlatan, traitor or loyal citizen, Fascist, anti-Semite, or just bewildered; poet or compiler—some have answered these questions for themselves, others consider them unanswerable. Was Pound's life tragic or farcical?

Political economists, literary critics, and psychologists will vie as to whose field is more competent to judge Pound at all. Indeed, the demand of strict aesthetes that Pound's work alone be the subject of literary criticism is hardly to be realized since the work itself does not confine itself within strictly aesthetic boundaries, but ever and again thrusts itself into the realm of politics.

What remains is a fragment, a torso. What remains is a man who never took the easy road. To compare his fate to that of Faust will be to find the answer. It is important to read Pound's poetry—to *read* Pound's *poetry.*

Ezra Pound, in the last analysis, is a phenomenon, an American phenomenon. Perhaps even a symptom. Seen from one vantage point it is clear that Pound's road in life was determined by his country, and that the road his country took, for him and against him, was determined by Pound's life. The errors of the one are mirrored in the failures of the other. Had it not been for the morally doubtful and dialectical interplay between accuser and accused, *The Pisan Cantos* could never have been written.

# *Notes*

Chapter 1

1. *Thus to Revisit* by Ford Madox Ford (London: Chapman and Hall, Ltd., 1929), p. 167. [Now issued by Octagon Books, New York.]
2. *Personae* (New York: New Directions, 1926), p. 46.
3. Quoted by William Van O'Connor and Edward Stone in *A Casebook on Ezra Pound* (New York: Thomas Y. Crowell & Co., 1959), p. 10.
4. *The Letters of Ezra Pound, 1907-1941,* edited by D. D. Paige (New York: Harcourt Brace & World, Inc., 1950), p. 182.
5. *Letters,* 1940, p. 341.
6. *Letters,* p. 340.
7. *Letters,* p. 345.
8. *Letters,* p. 48.
9. *ABC of Reading* (New Haven: Yale University Press, 1934), p. 84. [Now issued by New Directions.]

Chapter 2

1. *Letters,* pp. 123 f.
2. Quoted by Noel Stock, *Poet in Exile* (Manchester University Press, 1964), pp. 85f.
3. *Literary Essays of Ezra Pound* (New York: New Directions, 1954), p. 437.

4. Quoted by Charles Norman, *Ezra Pound: A Biography* (New York: Macmillan, 1960), p. 22. [Now issued by Funk and Wagnalls, New York.]

5. Ibid.

6. *Modern American Poetry, Modern British Poetry,* Combined Mid-Century Edition (New York: Harcourt, Brace and Co., 1950), p. 12.

7. Noel Stock (see 2 above), pp. 5f.

8. William Van O'Connor (see 3, Chapter 1), p. 11.

9. *Letters,* pp. 224 f.

10. Charles Norman (see 4 above), p. 70.


*Chapter 3*

1. Charles Norman (see 4, Chapter 2), p. 29.

2. Eustace Mullins, *This Difficult Individual, Ezra Pound* (New York: Fleet Publishing Corp., 1961), p. 37.

3. William Carlos Williams, *I Wanted To Write a Poem* (Boston: Beacon Press, 1958), p. 5.

4. Charles Norman (see 4, Chapter 2), p. 32.

5. Ibid., p. 33.

6. Ford Madox Ford, *New York Essays* (New York: William Edwin Rudge Inc., 1927), p. 35.

7. Canto LXXXII.

8. Charles Norman (see 4, Chapter 2), pp. 37f.

9. *Letters,* pp. 3f.

10. *Gaudier-Brzeska, a Memoir* (New York: New Directions, 1960), p. 85.

11. *Patria Mia* (Chicago: Ralph Fletcher Seymour, 1950), quote on p. 33.

12. Quoted by Hugh Kenner, *The Poetry of Ezra Pound* (New York: New Directions, 1951), p. 337.

13. George Dekker, *Sailing after Knowledge: The Cantos of Ezra Pound* (London, 1963), p. 126. [Issued by Barnes and Noble, New York, as *The Cantos of Ezra Pound.*]

14. *The Spirit of Romance* (London: Peter Owen Ltd., 1960), pp. 7f.
15. Richard Aldington, *Life for Life's Sake* (New York: The Viking Press, 1941), pp. 134f.
16. *Gaudier-Brzeska, a Memoir,* p. 82.
17. Ibid., p. 83.
18. *Letters,* pp. 9f.
19. Quoted by Stock (see 2, Chapter 2), p. 229.
20. *Gaudier-Brzeska, a Memoir,* p. 86.
21. Ibid., p. 89.
22. Eustace Mullins (see 2 above), p. 104.
23. Ibid., p. 105.

*Chapter 4*

1. Quoted by Alexander N. Jeffares, *W. B. Yeats, Man and Poet* (New York: Barnes and Noble, 1949), p. 167.
2. *Letters,* p. 41.
3. *Letters,* p. vii.
4. Hugh Kenner (see 12, Chapter 3), p. 109.
5. *Pound/Joyce,* edited by Forrest Read (New York: New Directions, 1967), pp. 268f.
6. William Van O'Connor (see 3, Chapter 1), p. 8.
7. *Letters,* p. 48.
8. Noel Stock (see 2, Chapter 2), pp. 64f.
9. Hugh Kenner (see 12, Chapter 3), p. 37.
10. Ibid., p. 45.
11. *Personae,* p. 126
12. Charles Norman (see 4, Chapter 2), p. 100.
13. "Allan Upward Serious," *New Age,* April 23, 1914.
14. "Murder by Capital," *The Criterion,* July, 1933.
15. Charles Norman, *The Case of Ezra Pound* (New York: Bodley Press, 1948), p. 32. [Now issued by Funk and Wagnalls, New York.]
16. William Van O'Connor (see 3, Chapter 1), p. 119.
17. Ibid.
18. *Letters,* p. 90.

19. *Letters,* p. 231.
20. George Dekker (see 13, Chapter 3), pp. 131f.
21. Op. cit., p. 96.


Chapter 5

1. William Van O'Connor (see 3, Chapter 1), p. 8.
2. *Letters,* p. 180.
3. *Letters,* p. 299.
4. Hugh Kenner (see 12, Chapter 3), p. 37.
5. *Letters,* p. 19.
6. *Letters,* p. 77.
7. *Letters,* p. 82.
8. *Letters,* p. 87.
9. *Letters,* p. 95.
10. *Letters,* p. 95.
11. *Letters,* p. 306.
12. *ABC of Reading* (see 9, Chapter 1), p. 34.
13. Ibid.
14. *Letters,* pp. 250f.
15. *The Annotated Index to the Cantos of Ezra Pound,* edited by John Edwards (Berkeley: University of California Press, 1957).
16. Op. cit., p. 200.
17. Carl Van Doren, *Benjamin Franklin* (New York: The Viking Press, 1952), p. 745.
18. Lore Lenberg, *Rosen aus Feilstaub* (Wiesbaden: Limes Verlag, 1966), pp. 188f.


Chapter 6

1. *Letters,* pp. 342f.
2. Charles Norman (see 15, Chapter 4), p. 35.
3. Pound's radio broadcasts are available at the Library of Congress, Washington, D.C.
4. Charles Norman (see 4, Chapter 2) p. 391.

5. From Canto LXXXI in *Cantos I to XCV* (New York: New Directions, 1965 rev. ed.).

6. Eustace Mullins (see 2, Chapter 3), p. 27.

7. Op. cit., p. 21.

8. William Van O' Connor (see 3, Chapter 1), p. 45.

# Chronology

1885: Ezra Pound born October 30 in Hailey, Idaho.

1887: Family moves to Wyncote, Pennsylvania.

1901–1905: College studies at the University of Pennsylvania and Hamilton College; B. A. from Hamilton in 1905.

1906: Master of Arts at University of Pennsylvania; fellowship and first trip to Europe.

1907: Teaches Romance languages and literature at Wabash College, Indiana.

1907–1908: Arrival in Italy. Publication of *A Lume Spento*.

1908: Arrival in London.

1909: *Personae. Exultations.* Lecturer at Regent St. Polytechnic.

1910: *The Spirit of Romance.*

1911: *Canzoni.*

1912: London correspondent for *Poetry* magazine. *Sonnets and Ballads of Guido Cavalcanti. Ripostes.*

1913: *Canzoni & Ripostes.* Imagist principles published in March issue of *Poetry*. Secretary to William Butler Yeats, 1913–14.

1914: Marriage to Dorothy Shakespear. *Des Imagistes.* Article on "Vorticism" in *Forthnightly Review*. *BLAST*.

1915: *Cathay.* Begins work on the *Cantos.*

1916: *Lustra.*

1918: *Pavannes and Divisions.*

1919: *Quia Pauper Amavi.* "Homage to Sextus Propertius."

1920: Arrival in Paris. "Hugh Selwyn Mauberley." Edits Eliot's "The Waste Land."

1921: *Poems* 1918–1921 (includes Cantos IV–VII). Articles on the economic theories of Douglas. Composes the opera, *Villon.*

1923: Studies in philosophy of Confucius.

1925: Arrival in Rappallo. *A Draft of XVI Cantos.*

1928: *Ta Hio. A Draft of Cantos 17–27.*

1930: *A Draft of XXX Cantos.*

1933: *ABC of Economics.*

1935: *Jefferson and/or Mussolini.*

1939: Visit to the U.S. Honorary doctorate from Hamilton College.

1940: Broadcasts for Radio Rome. *Cantos LII–LXXI.*

1943: Indicted for treason by the U.S.

1945: May through November, imprisonment at Pisa. Removal to Washington. New indictment.

1946: Committed to St. Elizabeth's Hospital as "of unsound mind."

1947: *The Unwobbling Pivot and The Great Digest* (Confucius), dated Pisa, October 5–November 5.

1948: *The Pisan Cantos* in *The Cantos of Ezra Pound.*

1949: Awarded the Bollingen Prize for Poetry.

1955: *Section Rock-Drill: 85–95 de los Cantares.*

1956: *Sophocles.*

1958: Treason charges dropped. Release from St. Elizabeth's. Arrival in Italy.

1959: *Thrones: 96–109 de los cantares.*

1963: *E. P. to L. U., Nine Letters written to Louis Untermeyer by Ezra Pound.*

1964: *Confucius to Cummings,* Anthology edited by Pound.

1968: *Drafts and Fragments of Cantos CX–CXVII.*

# Selected Bibliography

*Selected Works by Ezra Pound*

*A Lume Spento,* 1908
*The Spirit of Romance,* 1910
*Ripostes,* 1912
*The Sonnets and Ballate of Guido Cavalcanti* (translation),
    1912
*Cathay* (translation), 1915
*Lustra,* 1916
*Gaudier-Brzeska* (with Ernest Fenollosa), 1916
*Pavannes and Divagations,* 1918
*Quia Pauper Amavi,* 1919
*The Cantos,* 1919–68
*Hugh Selwyn Mauberley,* 1920
*Instigations,* 1921
*Indiscretions,* 1923
*Antheil and the Treatise on Harmony,* 1924
*Personae,* 1926
*Ta Hio* (translation), 1928
*Homage to Sextus Propertius* (translation), 1934
*Guide to Culture,* 1938
*The Unwobbling Pivot and The Great Digest* (translation
    of Confucius), 1947
*If This Be Treason,* 1948

*The Letters of Ezra Pound,* 1950
*The Confucian Analects* (translation), 1951
*The Confucian Odes: The Classic Anthology Defined by Confucius* (translation), 1954
*Cavalcanti Poems* (translation), 1966

*Critical Works on Ezra Pound*

Dembo, L. I. *The Confucian Odes of Ezra Pound: A Critical Appraisal.* 1963
Espey, John. *Ezra Pound's Mauberley: A Study in Composition.* 1955
Kenner, Hugh. *The Poetry of Ezra Pound.* 1951
Norman, Charles. *Ezra Pound: A Biography.* 1960
Stock, Noel. *Poet in Exile, Ezra Pound.* 1964

# Index

117